IMPROVING YOUR TENNIS

IMPROVING YOUR TENNIS
Strokes and Techniques

by

C. M. Jones

with action drawings by
Mike Herring

FABER AND FABER
3 Queen Square
London

First published in 1973
by Faber & Faber Limited
3 Queen Square London WC1
Reprinted 1974
Filmset and printed
in Great Britain by
BAS Printers Limited,
Wallop, Hampshire

ISBN 0 571 10148 8

Contents

Contents

Chapter One

Tennis—The Game

Tennis (singles) is a game played on a court in which one man (or woman—'man' is used from now on to mean a player of either sex) tries to place a ball in the other's half of that court so that (a) he cannot touch the ball or (b) he is unable to return the ball into the striker's half of the court.

In men's singles matches on modern court surfaces the ball crosses and recrosses the net on average around five times before one player either errs or hits an untouchable shot.

In women's singles the 'rallies' (the ball crossing and recrossing the net) normally continue for more shots—occasionally over 100 and in one memorable rally 474 times.

In doubles the 'alleys' or 'tramlines' running the length of each side of the court become effective.

The length of the court for either singles or doubles is 78 feet. The width for singles is 27 feet and that of each 'alley' $4\frac{1}{2}$ feet, so that the doubles court is 36 feet wide.

The service line is 21 feet from the net, which is 3 feet high at the centre and $3\frac{1}{2}$ feet high at posts standing 3 feet outside each sideline. So in doubles the posts have to be moved outside the alley. It is customary, however, for the posts to remain in the doubles positions and for temporary, spike-ended sticks to be put in each alley as supplementary net supports when singles are played.

There are three basic strokes in the game, namely—

    (1) Service.
    (2) Groundstrokes.
    (3) Volleys.

9

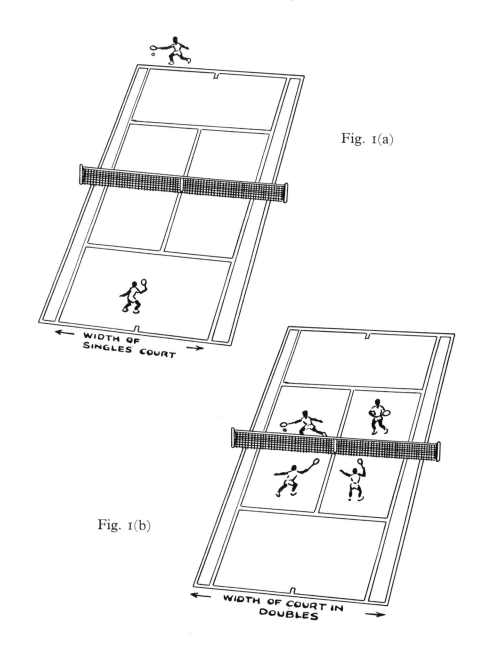

Fig. 1(a)

← WIDTH OF
SINGLES COURT →

Fig. 1(b)

← WIDTH OF COURT IN
DOUBLES →

A service starts each rally. It is made by the server throwing the ball in the air and then hitting it before it bounces into the service court diagonally across the net. If the first attempt fails (a fault) he is allowed a second chance. Points are played alternately from side A to service court A and side B to service court B.

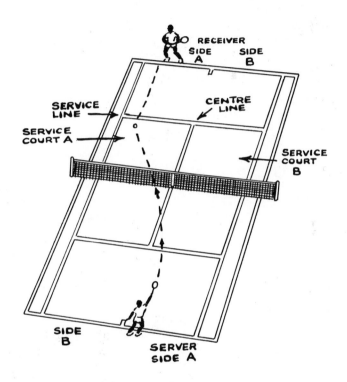

Fig. 2

Volleys are strokes made before the ball bounces in the striker's court. The ball must be allowed to bounce when receiving service but all other returns may be volleyed.

However, for technical and tactical reasons most volleys are made in the area between the service line and the net.

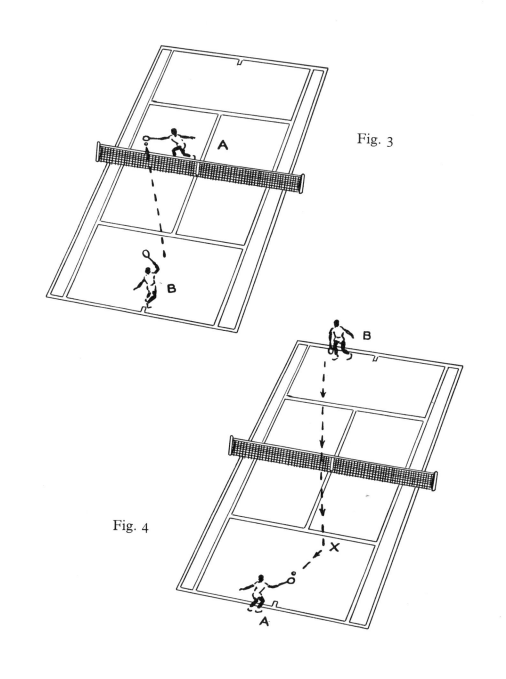

Fig. 3

Fig. 4

Strokes struck after allowing the ball to bounce are categorised 'groundstrokes'. They can be made within a few feet of the net if one man drops the ball very close to the net but they are usually played somewhere near the baseline.

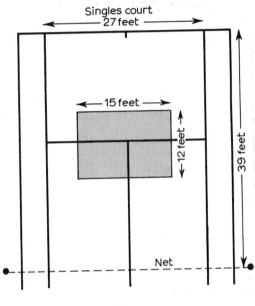

Fig. 5

In singles you and your opponent are each covering half a court, dimensions 13 yards long by 9 yards wide, total 117 square yards.

How strange, therefore, that something like 80 per cent of shots hit by players in singles matches up to and even including Wimbledon standard land the ball in a rectangle approximately 5 yards by 4 yards, or 20 square yards in all (see shaded area on Fig. 5). Thus they are wasting 80 per cent of the area open to their placements.

The moral, therefore, is to learn to hit the ball into the six key areas marked on Fig. 6. Each one is approximately 3 feet by 3 feet.

Start aiming every shot for them from the first time you play tennis so that placing becomes habitual. It is *never* too early to develop this habit.

Of course all the court should be exploited but if you master hitting 90 per cent of your shots into A or B you will be very difficult to beat.

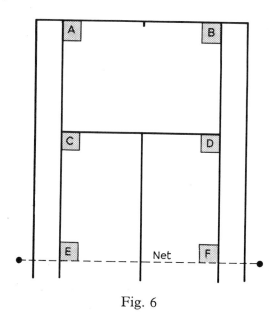

Fig. 6

Except at the first Wimbledon in 1877—and perhaps even this was not really an exception—the service has been regarded as an aggressive shot with which to win points. . . . And in three ways—

(1) By sending over such a fast and well placed ball the receiver cannot get his racket to it; these are called ACES.

(2) By speed and placing which, though the receiver gets racket to ball, allows him no chance of returning it; these are called SERVICE WINNERS.

(3) By serving so effectively the receiver can only return the ball weakly for the server to make a winning stroke.

14

Sheer speed is not sufficient. The ball has to be placed well. The most effective areas are shown in Fig. 7. CR and WR when serving from the right of the centre mark on the baseline, CL and WL when serving from the left.

When you begin you will be lucky to hit a tablecloth placed in any of those positions. Later, a large tea tray may prove difficult but

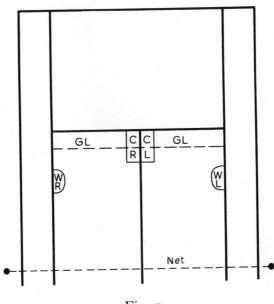

Fig. 7

after a lot of practice you can start using a handkerchief or tennis ball box as your target.

Nevertheless, you will always serve some balls which go into the net or outside the service court—'faults'—and you will have to deliver the second ball. You may be skilled enough to hit or confident enough to try for the same target areas but whether or not you are, you should be concerned with length—a good second service should fall in a narrow strip about a foot wide, shown on the diagram as the area GL (for good length).

Have you yet considered or discovered what the other symbols mean? CR and CL mean centre right or left, WR and WL wide right or left.

If you watch tennis in a public park it will seem that most services merely start the rally. So let us instead examine those used by the game's great servers—men like Maurice McLoughlin in the early 1900s, Bill Tilden in the 1920s, Ellsworth Vines in the 1930s, Pancho Gonzales in the 1950s and Stan Smith, Arthur Ashe or Vladimir Zednik in the 1960s and 1970s.

All these men—and women like Virginia Wade—have one thing in common. What is it?

One final sentence before moving on. Throughout the book I will be making comparisons in effects caused by variations of details. In all cases the comparison assumes all other factors remain equal.

BASIC CONCEPTIONS

There are three basic 'feels' to the strokes one uses in tennis, namely—

For service, of throwing the racket at the ball.

For groundstrokes, of swinging the racket at the ball.

For volleys, of punching the ball.

These expressions will come up time and again so try fully to understand what they mean. . . . And not merely in the brain.

Tennis is properly regarded as an intellectual as well as an athletic game. It is necessary to understand and think about what is happening but unless you really feel it in the middle of your stomach, you will not progress very far.

So to develop your service power, practise throwing a ball. Seek rhythm, be careful in the timing of weight transference into the throw, develop a strong wrist flick because this is what converts a fast service into an unreturnable cannon ball.

Record the increases in your power by measuring the distance you can throw a ball. Better, get hold of an old racket and throw that instead of a ball. Take time over the wind up and then let the power flow into your throw.

WHOLE OR PART?

In learning ground shots arm a friend with a couple of dozen tennis balls and have him throw them, one at a time, so you are kept moving around the court as if in a match. Hit those balls for the corners and not back to your friend. Simulate rally play as faithfully as you can in order to obtain maximum 'transference' from a training to competitive situation. Remember to swing your racket.

In learning to volley 'part' methods may prove beneficial but, as soon as you can, learn by hitting an approach shot before running in to punch your volley—probably another ball thrown by your coach or friend. But how valuable can coaching be?

Wilfred Rhodes, that great England and Yorkshire cricketer, was once heard to say, 'Coaching is important, very important. But tha can't put in what God left out.'

Wise words though these may be, they beg one question of supreme importance and that is to discover with any certainty what it is God has indeed left out of any particular person.

At first glance a whole range of vital factors may be missing—a good sense of timing, rhythmic movement, co-ordination, a true eye, rapid reflexes, etc. etc.

But long experience has taught me—often the hard way—that an apparent deficiency need not be an actual one. It is safer to assume a complex intermingling of genetics and environment—nature and nurture—and so adopt the positive and optimistic idea that most things are possible. 'The impossible we achieve quickly; miracles take a little longer.'

There are, of course, some well-defined practical limits to this approach. For example, the chances of a small, light-weight woman like Joyce Williams attaining a proficiency in the serve and volley 'big game' of an Amazon like Margaret Court are far from good. But this need not—does not—prevent Mrs Williams from serving and volleying adequately, while running up some special 'plus values' of her own such as outstanding mobility and fleetness of foot. In learning, therefore, there is no case for believing anything is impossible until it has been well and truly attempted.

How should that learning come about? Should a stroke be broken down into a number of constituent factors—part learning—or tackled as a complete unit right from the start—whole learning?

Because tennis is a game of fluid movement, flowing strokes and a moving ball I believe first the strokes and then the common tactical situations should normally be learned by the 'whole' system.

There will be occasions where 'part' learning can be advantageously adopted and adapted to special needs.

Since the printed word and picture are static, try to read and visualise all that follows in a moving form. The techniques are only means towards the end of controlling the ball and ultimately winning the point.

Yes, controlling the ball and winning the point because the former leads to the latter and if you gain sufficient of the latter, victory will be yours. In tennis as in nature, tall oaks from little acorns grow.

Chapter Two

The Strokes—Service

America has produced more cannonball servers than any other country. The great national game there is baseball and nearly all children—boys AND girls—play it from the earliest possible age. Many like to become good batters but more seek to gain fame as pitchers and all have to throw the ball around the field.

See the connection? No? Well, the secret of good serving lies in throwing the racket head at the ball. First throw the ball itself.

Fig. 8

Then find an old racket, stand about 6 yards from the side or back netting of the court and throw the racket at the netting.

Then take a ball in your left hand (if you are a right-handed player) and as you start a throwing action with your racket (don't let go this time) place the ball in position so that the racket 'throw' connects with the ball and propels it in the direction of your opponent's service court.

Fig. 9

Forget about all refinements for the moment. Simply concentrate on throwing your racket at the ball. Once you can connect a powerful 'throw' with the ball you will have started to learn a good service.

How powerful is 'powerful'. Well, if you stand in the normal serving position and throw that old racket, it should, if you let it go, clear the net and land deep in your opponents court. However, there are methods for adding power to a basically good technique. The length of the backswing before the elbow 'breaks' into the throwing position affects both power and control. Both are dependent on the length of time the moving racket head stays on the same line the ball is travelling. Fig. 10 shows how wrist action helps this.

20

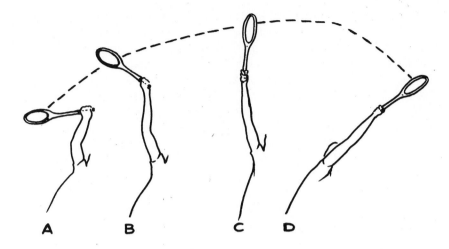

Fig. 10

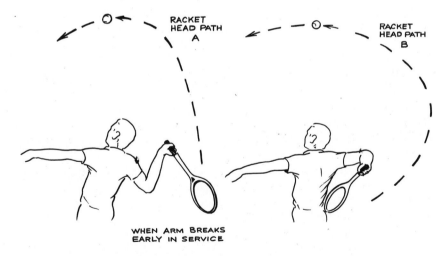

Fig. 11(a)

Fig. 11(b)

Now look at Fig. 11. In (a) the 'break' comes early and the path travelled by the racket head changes rapidly near the point of impact. In (b) the arm travels farther backwards before the break, resulting in the racket head taking a more circular and regular path to impact. Fig. 11(c) approximates the angles during the critical foot or so before correction. In *Tennis: How to Become a Champion* I showed how this increased power proportionally to the cosine of the angle. Though this is a considerable over-simplification, the point remains fundamentally valid.

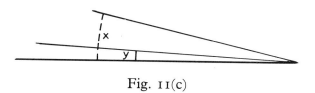

Fig. 11(c)

What is much more apparent from the drawings is that path (A) needs a much finer control than path (B) if the ball is to be hit at the correct angle to send it into the opponent's court.

Thus if there are two servers exactly matched in all talents, but with one 'breaking' as in drawing (a) and the other as in drawing (b), (b) must have marked superiority in accuracy and consistency to (a), pace for pace of delivery.

Thus the farther back you can swing your arm before 'breaking' for the throw, the more effective your service is likely to be.

Another important aspect of the swing back lies in the way the racket strings are faced. Turn to Fig. 18 on page 30 and notice in drawing (a) how the striking face of the racket is 'looking' at the server.

In Fig. 18 (b) it is still 'looking' at the server although it has begun to twist slightly in a clockwise direction to 'peep' up the court. The technical term for a racket face which 'looks' at the server is 'closed racket face'.

A few moments of experimental racket swinging (out of doors, please, electric bulbs are expensive) will reveal much more convincingly than words how keeping the racket face closed as long as possible on the backswing helps to deepen and strengthen the throwing action, so increasing power. For the moment let us dwell upon control.

Think for a moment. Can the racket strings exercise any influence on the ball if they are not actually in contact? Clearly, the answer must be 'no' (Fig. 12).

How does a human being 'feel' a tennis ball hit the racket strings? The sensory nerves respond to the impact by transmitting electrical

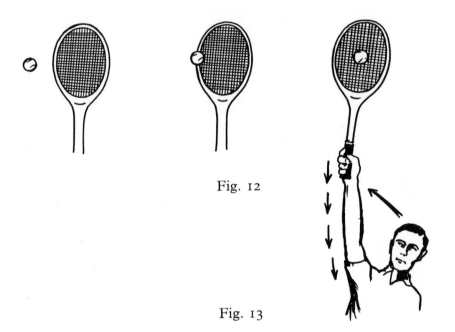

Fig. 12

Fig. 13

impulses to the brain. There the information is 'processed' and appropriate orders for muscular movements are fed back via the nervous system to the relevant muscles (Fig. 13).

The message of impact travels to the brain by electrical impulses, NOT as a continuous wave of energy. It is difficult, if not impossible to strengthen the impulses, only to increase the number.

Therefore, the longer the ball is in contact with the strings, the greater will be the number of impulses and, consequently the more intense the 'feel'. Thus 'touch' players need slacker string rackets— say around 53 lb.—than power players—say 63 lb.—all other things being equal (this is somewhat over simplified). But power demands maximum acceleration being given to the ball. With a constant pressure, constant speed, constant swing of racket, added acceleration can only come from the elasticity of frame and gut.

Frame elasticity is a complex subject and so is gut. Broadly speaking, fine gauge lamb's gut possesses the greatest elasticity but it has a shorter life than man-made fibres of minimal elasticity.

So gut quality and stringing tension are not merely a question of playing preferences but also of economics. To the rich player or one who receives rackets free of charge there is no problem. To the moderate income, young family man compromise is essential.

The force imparted on both ball and gut is dramatically shown in this picture (Fig. 14c) of a badminton racket at the moment of

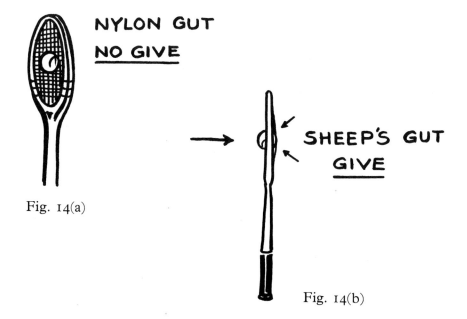

NYLON GUT
NO GIVE

SHEEP'S GUT
GIVE

Fig. 14(a)

Fig. 14(b)

impact with a shuttlecock. A shuttlecock is much harder than a tennis ball yet it still suffers considerable distortion before being catapulted back across the net.

Fig. 14(c)

Around the turn of the century inventive American players evolved a number of variations of the basic service, some of which became and remain strong offensive weapons today.

Heading the list is the American twist service, shown in Figs. 15 and 16 comparing the top spin and twist deliveries.

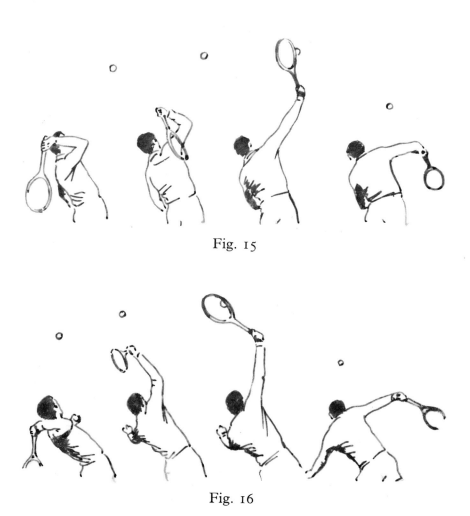

Fig. 15

Fig. 16

In the top spin service the ball is 'placed' in position slightly to the right and the racket head is 'thrown' straight through the ball.

In the twist service the back bend is considerable and the ball is 'placed' up behind the head. By vigorously straightening the back and using a severe, left to right, wrist flick the ball is spun viciously in a clockwise direction, viewed from behind as in the pictures.

This spin causes the ball to swerve in flight and to kick after bouncing. The degree of swerve and the height and viciousness of the kick depends on the explosive power of the back straightening and of the wrist snap (Fig. 16).

If these are as severe as were those of Maurice McLoughlin back in 1913, the ball will swerve slightly from left to right, kick to head height and break sharply away to the right as viewed by the server.

Few men, however, possess the flexibility, power and skill to achieve this degree of spin. Thus, the normal twist serve travels in roughly a straight line, or even with a right to left swerve, and kicks only to about shoulder height.

Fig. 17

These variations in flight are caused by differing degrees and angles of spin. In a perfect American twist service, the spin of the ball is markedly more lateral than forward. This ratio of lateral to forward spin not only governs the swerve in flight but also the degree of kick and break of the ball.

When the lateral spin component is pronounced the ball jerks upwards after bouncing much more sharply than when the forward spin component is stronger. Then the kick is less vicious and the bound of the ball is forward rather than from left to right.

This application of spin is shown in the drawings of the top spin service. Note the direction of the racket follow through.

In producing spin services pronounced body turn is usually desirable (see Fig. 17).

Players of the calibre and tactical skill of Jaroslav Drobny deliberately vary the pace and spins of their services, running through every mixture between the extremes set out in this chapter.

The laws of tennis allow the server two tries to deliver a ball into court. Consequently, a preponderance of players lash at the first ball with all their might and when, as happens three-quarters of the time, it is a 'fault'—into the net or beyond the boundaries of the service court or, perhaps, a foot-fault—they tap the second over weakly, hoping that the opponent will not murder it.

It is said among the top world stars, 'a player is only as good as his second service,' and while this may be a considerable over-simplification there is still a good deal of truth in the words.

Apart from any measurable superiority of a man's first service over his second—pace, length, placement, etc.—there is also a significant psychological advantage. The receiver knows the server must get the second ball in court or else waste the point in the manner of a cricketer delivering a 'no ball' and so he, the receiver, can apply considerable pressure by adopting a menacing stance and taking up a clearly agressive position. Thus he is ready to take advantage of the weaker second service and also increase the chances of it being weaker by perfectly legal intimidation.

So never unthinkingly waste a first service. There will be times when desperation or the score or the need to disturb the composure of a confident opponent demands an attempt to deliver a fast, well placed service which he cannot touch—an 'ace'. But these will be outnumbered by five or six or more other occasions when the best course is to come down to 80 per cent of top speed in order to give that first service every chance of going into play.

Length is all important. Remember the laws of tennis are such that the service ball must bounce before the receiver may hit it so even a slow service pitched right up to the service line cannot easily be blasted into oblivion by the receiver.

Add a modicum of spin, pace and deception and, with the right kind of backing, your service will be extremely difficult to break. France's Jean Borotra, whose play in the 1920s undoubtedly secured him tennis immortality, had, in isolation, a far inferior service to many a woman, including Margaret Court as a prime example. But it was so long, so varied in placement and so controlled in speed that Borotra, the 'Bounding Basque', was able to run in behind it to such ideal volleying positions that he was possibly the hardest man to pass at the net the game has ever known.

Fig. 18 shows the basic service action in considerable detail, beginning with the starting position. The eyes are looking at the opponent, the racket pointing at him, the left hand supporting the racket at its throat. The left foot is directed along the intended line of delivery, the right turned about 35° clockwise from the left.

Note that the right wrist is relaxed and not cocked stiffly upwards. This wrist relaxation is essential if the racket head is to be thrown viciously into the hit.

To test the truth of this go through your throwing action without hitting a ball or letting go of the racket, first with the wrist locked, then with it relaxed and adding speed to the throwing action. With the wrist locked, the strings make little noise. With it relaxed and giving acceleration, the strings cutting through the air make a loud 'swish'. The faster the acceleration, the louder the 'swish' so it is possible to judge potential power simply by listening.

The second picture shows the start of the action, with the two arms making a scissoring movement, the left upwards, the right downwards.

Note that the left arm is pushing or placing the ball up for the hit rather than throwing. Note, too, that the arm and left shoulder are turning to the right so that body weight may later be exploded into the hit.

The server is keeping his left side pulled in. Many novices let it stick out, thus ruining balance and setting up a percentage chance of torn stomach or side muscles, both painful and slow healing conditions.

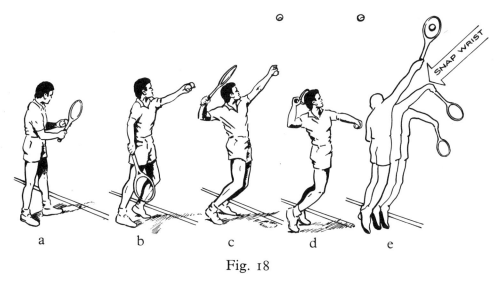

Fig. 18

The knees are bending, thus helping a power-adding upwards and twisting thrust at impact. The combined body turn and knees dip permits a 'rising spiral' action, the most powerful possible in a human being.

Pictures (c) and (d) show the throwing action developing. The knees continue to relax and the body to swivel. The head is held up and the eyes focus on the ball.

Picture (e) shows impact and immediately after and spotlights the powerful wrist snap which converted the model's service from fast into cannonball.

Look at the right leg. It is still grounded and behind the left leg, thus ensuring the hit is being made from a firm base. Far too many servers allow their body and leg to turn in and go past the optimum power position ahead of the hit, thus sacrificing speed, accuracy and length. Spin, too, reduces pace proportionally to the amount applied. In this case there is. . . But look for yourself. Is there any spin being imparted? Clearly not. The racket head has travelled straight through the ball.

Key points to remember in the flat, cannonball service are—
(1) Sideways to the net.
(2) Slow 'build up' to the swing; have you ever watched a labourer breaking a large stone with a long-handled, 14-lb. hammer? He uses a slow build up before hurling full power into the downward hit.
(3) Careful 'placing up' of the ball assists balance.
(4) Swivel body and straighten knees into the hit, not ahead of it.
(5) Hit ball at the top of full stretch.
There is no semblance of a 'foot fault' in the service, even under the old laws. Today the umpire or linesman or, if there is one, foot fault judge may call you if law 7 is broken. This reads—

'The server shall throughout the delivery of the service: (a) not change his position by walking or running; (b) not touch with either foot, any area other than that behind the baseline within the imaginary extension of the centre mark and side-line.'

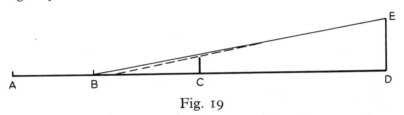

Fig. 19

Should the ball be hit above, along, or below an imaginary line joining the point of impact between ball and racket and the point on the opponent's court where the ball is supposed to land?

Fig. 19 is a side view of a tennis court surface where length A to D is from baseline to baseline. B represents the service line, C the net at the centre band (3 feet high) and E the hitting point of a service delivered by a man about 6¼ feet tall. The plan is to scale.

The straight line from E to service line B clears the top of the net by approximately 9 inches.

The broken line, which just clears the net, lands the ball 3 feet inside the service line.

Deduct 6 inches from the server's height—making him or her $5\frac{3}{4}$ feet tall—and a straight line which clears the net falls beyond service line B. So very few women can serve the ball in a straight line from impact to touch down within an opponents service court; remember, the net is $3\frac{1}{2}$ feet high at the posts, so that worsens the 'mathematics'.

There is not the slightest need to worry about this, as *Lawn Tennis* magazine proved in an article by D. A. D. Cooke, MA, Graduate Member, I. Mech. E., in the September 1970 issue. The relevant passages in his article read:

'What the author was interested in finding were the angles of inclination between which a server of a given height and serving at a given speed had to hit the ball in order that it would go over the net but not over the service baseline. Some of the questions which this calculation would answer were: Is a short server at a great disadvantage compared with a tall one? When the ball is served, is it hit above or below the horizontal direction? And is there a serving speed above which it is not possible to get the ball into court? All relate to flat services.

'Results are shown graphically [Fig. 20]. Angles in the figures are degrees above the horizontal at which the tennis ball leaves the racket, and the upper and lower set of contours are respectively the angles above which the ball goes over the line and below which the ball goes into the net. Therefore for a player to make a good service the ball must be struck so as to come between the full and dotted line corresponding to his height. The top line in each set of contours is for a server whose height is $4\frac{1}{2}$ feet, the middle line for one of $5\frac{3}{4}$ feet and the lowest line for one of 7 feet. The speed scale extends to 140 m.p.h. but a faster service of 154 m.p.h. has been recorded (M. J. Sangster —1963). Contours only go down as far as 40 m.p.h. because a 30 m.p.h. service will not go over the baseline no matter what angle it is served at, and a 20 m.p.h. service will not go over the net.

'To give an example of how the graph works let us examine what happens at 40 m.p.h. and 140 m.p.h. with servers of $4\frac{1}{2}$ feet and 7 feet. At the lower speed and for the short player the ball will be out over the line if it is hit at more than $13 \cdot 6°$ above the horizontal and into the net if hit at less than 5·8° above the horizontal. To get the ball into the service box then the allowable margin is (13·6–5·8) =7·8°. For the 7 feet player the margin is (12·5–3·6)=8·9°. At the higher service speed the margins are (−4·5−(−5·0))=0·4° for the short server and (−6·6−(−8·3))=1·7° for the tall one. Thus for slow services the short server is at very little disadvantage compared with the tall one, but for fast services he has to be up to 1·7/0·4 or 4·25 times as accurate. The graph also shows that the ball must leave the racket in an upward direction for slow services and downward for fast ones. At intermediate speeds the ball leaves the racket approximately horizontally.

'For those interested in technical details the computations were done by an IBM 1130 computer. The sums take into account air

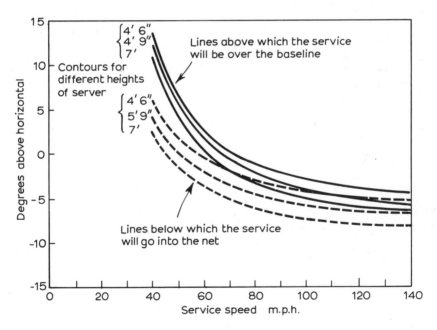

Fig. 20

resistance but not spinning of the ball. In practice top and side spin of a tennis ball make it dip more sharply, requiring serving to be less accurate. Spin, however, is not expected to affect the overall pattern.

'Air resistance is a very important factor in calculating the flight path of a ball, and cannot be ignored even though the time between serving a ball and its bouncing on the other side of the net may be as little as a third of a second. For instance, in the fastest service ever recorded, when the ball left the racket at 154 m.p.h., the ball was only travelling at 108 m.p.h. when it crossed the net, and its initial deceleration was about 9g.

'Normally two competitors would not vary by more than about 9 inches in height and the advantage that the taller man then has is not more than 40 per cent. Therefore the main conclusion of these calculations is that a short server is not at a very great disadvantage compared with a tall one.

'A service, however, must become more accurate as its speed increases. For a $5\frac{3}{4}$ feet server the allowable margin decreases progressively from $8\cdot4°$ to $1\cdot1°$ as the speed increases from 40 to 140 m.p.h.

'The use of slice counters this disadvantage markedly, the spin pulling the ball down slightly during its flight, so compensating for the angular factors arising from height differentials.

'This is the practical reason why small men like R. L. Riggs, who won the Wimbledon singles in 1939, suffered no pronounced service liability compared with his main rival of the immediate pre-war years, J. D. Budge, who is approximately 9 inches taller than Riggs.'

Spin can be applied to service in a number of ways but in current tennis only three are in general use, namely slice, top spin and American twist. All three tend to pull the ball down into court, thus giving a wider margin of safety than hitting the ball without spin (flat).

Slice swerves the ball in flight from right to left and then makes it keep low after bouncing.

Top spin causes little curve in flight but makes the ball bound high and long after hitting the ground.

34

American twist, if correctly applied, swerves the ball from left to right in flight and then causes it to break away to the right and kick upwards after bouncing.

In actual play, few servers apply either top spin or American twist in text book fashion so that curve in flight and post-bounce behaviour of the ball both vary considerably from the specification just given. Both top spin and twist demand considerable back flexibility and strength if they are really to menace the receiver. If such services are only half-hearted they become liabilities rather than assets so master the slice first.

SERVICE CHECK POINTS

(a) Ball going in net

(1) Throw-up of ball too low.
(2) Throw-up of ball too far forward.
(3) Looking to see where ball is going before impact.
(4) Right leg coming forward too soon.
(5) Hurrying to follow ball to net instead of letting the service action pull you naturally into a foward run.
(6) Not stretching up to full height for service.
(7) Hurrying the first part of the swing.
(8) Hitting down at ball. Unless you are well over 6 feet tall you must hit the ball upwards.

(b) Ball too long

(1) Throw-up too far back.
(2) Arm bent and under ball to compensate for low throw-up.
(3) Body weight back and not moving into ball.
(4) Loss of balance during the service.
(5) Hand slipping round behind the handle during the swing.
(6) Pushing ball instead of hitting it.
(7) Hurrying the first part of the swing.

(c) *Ball travelling too much to your left*

(1) Wrist not twisting to let strings 'look' at court at moment of impact.
(2) Body pivoting into service ahead of the hit.
(3) Stance too square to the net.
(4) Throw-up too far forward and too much to the right.

(d) *Lack of power*

(1) Poor timing, probably through hurrying the backswing.
(2) Not truly throwing racket at ball.
(3) Not imparting wrist snap.
(4) Body weight going into swing ahead of actual hit.
(5) Grip too far behind handle.
(6) Stretching to full height too soon.

Chapter Three

Groundstrokes

THE FOREHAND DRIVE

At least once in every rally of two or more returns the ball has to be struck after it has bounced. Such returns are named 'groundstrokes', those hit on the right of the body of a right-handed player being called 'forehand' drives, those on the left hand side 'backhands'.

When primitive men fought for survival they punched from their right-hand sides and so some collective, inherited subconscious causes beginners to start by hitting from this side. So the forehand drive is generally regarded as the 'natural' stroke but this does not make it the easiest one.

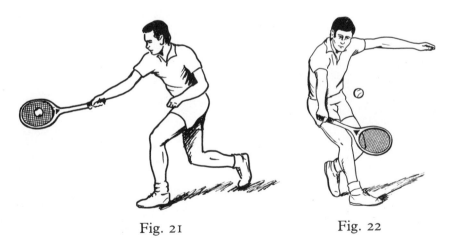

Fig. 21   Fig. 22

However, because of its fighting ancestry, it remains the most aggressive one and so it must be tackled immediately. However, the backhand drive should be learnt simultaneously.

There are an almost infinite number of ways of holding the racket for a forehand drive but the most commonly used by advanced players is known as the Eastern or 'shake hands' grip.

To obtain this, hold a racket by the throat with the butt of the handle pointing at your navel, the handle parallel with the ground and the cross-strings of the head at right angles to the ground.

Place your right hand flat against the strings (right-hand side of the racket face), slide it down the handle to the butt and then shake hands with the handle. Clearly, there will be tiny individual differences in the actual way each player will end up gripping his racket.

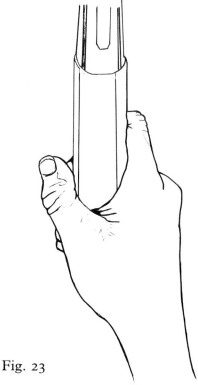

Fig. 23

These differences are not immensely important but the amount of feel you obtain in your fingers is. So after obtaining the basic grip in the way just decribed, shuffle your fingers slightly until the racket feels an extension of your arm and hand.

This is important because the effect of a forehand drive hit with a true Eastern grip is of the racket face resembling the fleshy part of the palm of the hand slapping the ball back over the net. Indeed, to get the idea, ask a friend to throw a ball to you, let it bounce and then slap it back for him to catch. Try quite a number and make a mental note of which part of the palm gives the best results. Usually it will be near the base of the fingers but wherever it is, that is likely to be the part of the hand which should be centred behind the racket handle.

The average, basic forehand drive is hit when the ball is around $2\frac{3}{4}$ feet above ground level. The net is, at its lowest point, 3 feet high, so, point one, the ball must be hit in an upward plane; in other words, lifted over the net though you will learn later that, in tennis, the word 'lifted' possesses a special meaning.

However, to ensure you remember this, say to yourself repeatedly before matches and often between points—

The main and primary object of the game of Lawn Tennis is to hit the ball over the net.

Supplement this by touching the court with the tip of your racket every time you settle down to receive a service. This will remind you to bend your knees and so get your racket down below the height at which it will strike the ball. This will assist the lifting action. Back in the 1500s they called the game from which tennis developed 'jeu de paume' (hand ball) and the best forehand drives today make the racket look like an extension of the striker's hand.

Turn now to Fig. 24. In drawing (a) the player has seen the ball is coming to his forehand side and has swung his racket back in preparation for the forward swing and hit. His weight is evenly balanced, his head well down so that his eyes can keep the ball constantly in view.

In (b) that forward swing has begun, his body weight is beginning a forward movement on to the front foot, and the face of the racket is slightly below the height at which the ball will be struck.

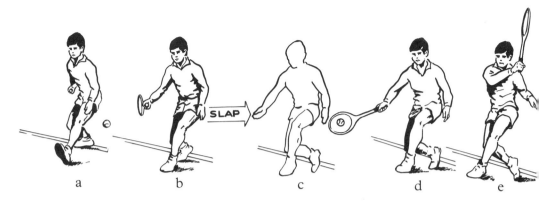

a   b   c   d   e

Fig. 24

Minus a racket he would hit the ball as in (c) but this is virtually the same as (d). The wrist is braced and firm, the shoulder has pivoted into the hit, body weight has swung through on to the front foot.

His head and shoulders are well down, so helping to keep the ball in view. This is extremely important because the head and shoulders exercise great influence on body control; more mistakes are made at tennis, golf and cricket through jerking the head up too soon to see where the ball has gone than through all other faults lumped together. The head pulls the shoulders up, this gives the swing an exaggerated rise and the ball flies upwards, clearing the opposite baseline in tennis or sending up an easy catch at cricket. If the striker is excessively over anxious, the jerk may be so violent and early that the implement sails over the top of the ball completely, resulting in the air shot of golf or the 'clean bowled' of cricket.

The head position should be as in (e), eyes still looking at the point of impact between racket and ball though the racket has followed through round and over the left shoulder. The knees are bent, the body weight well forward and the left arm is assisting body balance.

Body balance is important on all shots and it can be developed to some degree by standing on a plank pivoting on a paint tin, or something similarly rounded, in the manner of a childs see-saw (Fig. 25). Exercising on this also strengthens leg muscles as well as helping to improve body balance.

Fig. 25   Fig. 26

That basic forehand involved no running into position. However, one is seldom allowed to hit a drive, forehand or backhand, without having to run. So the most used forehand drive is struck with the feet and body nearly or quite parallel with the net (Fig. 26).

In the first picture of the sequence drawings (Fig. 27) the player has begun to move rapidly to a wide return and in the second is nearing the end of the backswing. The third and fourth show how shoulder and body weight are thrown into the drive, the left leg coming forward to take the thrust.

Note how the knees are flexible and bent and the eyes, through steadiness of head and shoulders, never lose sight of the ball.

The shoulders and hips are parallel with the baseline at the moment of impact, contrary to much theoretical teaching of the past.

Turning the body into the forehand drive early helps in making the racket travel along the same line as the ball during impact, so

41

Fig. 27

increasing slightly the time in which the ball and racket strings remain in contact. This allows more contact impulses to travel from hand to brain and so assists control. The Americans call this 'staying with the ball' (see Fig. 28). This also assists power.

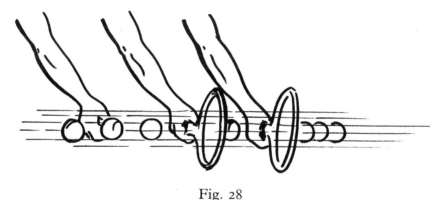

Fig. 28

Note, too, that the player is in full forward movement and so can easily continue a run to the net if the situation suggests this to be desirable.

In rally play one is normally forced to run continuously along the baseline from sideline to sideline. Consequently, the body weight flow is at a 90° angle from the direction of the hit. Furthermore,

Fig. 29

there is usually not enough time to position the feet as for the basic drive and, even if there were, the stroke would be clumsy.

So a slightly different tehnique is necessary. This necessitates a deliberate rotation of the body in order to transfer body mass into the hit and an exaggerated thrust in the follow-through to compensate for the loss of momentum caused through its being at right angles (90°) to the direction the ball is being aimed. This technique is exemplified in Fig. 29.

There are two definite advantages in this open stance technique. Firstly, one is able to reach farther and so, as in the drawings, pull the ball across the court; with a left foot forward technique in this situation it would be extremely difficult to hit the ball anywhere but down the line.

Secondly, an open stance used in conjunction with early body rotation as shown helps the racket to travel markedly along the line of aim during the vital 12 inches of 'zip' area just before and after the moment of impact. Consequently, the strings and ball remain in contact marginally longer, so increasing touch sensations, leading to better control and, if desired, greater power.

THE BACKHAND DRIVE

Deal yourself a pack of cards. . . . Or throw your hat into a chair. . . . Or throw a hoopla ring over a cup on the table.

OK. So now you know why the backhand drive is the easiest of all tennis shots to learn. . . . And why, if you go to Wimbledon and are able to hurry round the courts to see all the 224 acceptances for the men's and women's singles in action, 200 will be stronger on the backhand than the forehand.

Why, then, do so many instructional books and the two television series made recently seem to make it all so difficult? Heaven alone knows, unless it is pure animal instinct taking control instead of the trained brain.

After all, if you get in a fight and have to punch you don't use a backhand. And at the Schoolboys' Exhibition some years ago I checked 127 boys who had never played before when they picked up a racket and swung it at a ball. All 127 tried to hit it with the forehand. . . . The old fight or flight syndrome taking over again.

So now you should understand why 'doing what comes naturally' cannot always be trusted. In a 'fight or flight' situation, punching is instinctive. Yet in a situation demanding skill and dexterity—card dealing or hoop throwing—the brain takes over and the backhand is chosen.

Now to convert this skill into a tennis stroke.

In throwing the hat or dealing the cards the action 'pulls' the missile and Françoise Durr, the famous French woman player, has shown that a racket can effectively be 'pulled' at the ball in a similar manner. Nevertheless, 999 out of every 1,000 players need a little more bracing of the wrist. So they turn the grip more on top of the racket handle so that their thumbs can go diagonally across or even straight along the back of the handle.

The most commonly used grip, then, is one which turns the hand very slightly from right to left on the handle, with the racket face and strings at right angles to the ground.

The 'V' formed by the thumb and forefinger centres on the diagonal bevel which joins the back flat of the handle to the top flat. Remember, on the forehand the 'V' is on the other bevel linking the top flat of the handle to the other upright flat.

Fig. 30 shows the end of the racket with the line running through it from top to bottom representing the racket face. FD is the direction the ball travels when hit with the forehand and BD, the direction for backhand drives or volleys. The arrows B and F show approximately where the 'V' of thumb and forefinger is positioned with the grips most commonly used by tournament players.

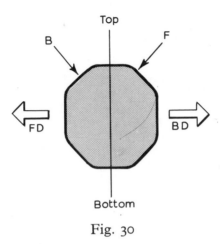

Fig. 30

Fig. 31 shows the thumb diagonally across the back of the handle. There is pressure between the thumb and first finger. Further support comes from the top part of the other three fingers. Remembering that the tips of the fingers are the most sensitive 'feelers' human beings possess, one can understand how this grip accentuates touch and, therefore, control. This is further helped if the first finger is spread slightly from the other fingers.

The complete adaptation of hat throwing to the backhand drive can now be understood (Fig. 32).

The racket is heavier than a playing card or hat. Thus most players use two hands for the backswing and many keep the left hand on the handle until very close to the moment of impact. The drawings clearly show how the backswing naturally turns your body away from the ball in readiness to pivot the weight forward into the hit.

Note that the hand is somewhat over the top of the handle, with

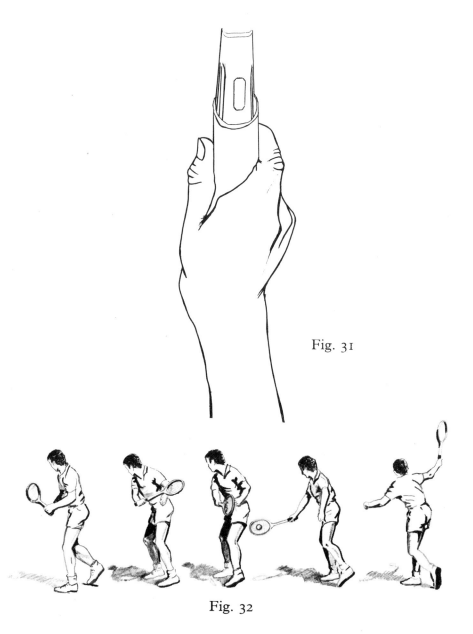

Fig. 31

Fig. 32

the thumb behind the handle to assist thrust. 'Feel' is obtained from pressure between the thumb and first finger.

Remember that, as with the forehand, the ball must be hit upwards if it is to clear the net barrier, so the plane taken by the racket face runs from below to above the meeting place of racket and ball.

Additional power is developed by stepping towards the ball during the forward swing. The racket face should follow through along the direction of the hit almost as though it is trying to 'chase' the ball over the net.

Brace the wrist whilst swinging the racket through the 'zip' area (roughly 6 inches either side of point of impact) and on no account let it make an involuntary, anti-clockwise turn so that the strings slide under the ball. There may be a case for occasionally 'slicing' in that manner deliberately but never for doing so involuntarily.

Hold the head and eyes well down until the follow through is complete and bend your knees to reach down for balls which skid through at a low altitude.

You are likely to hear repeatedly the expression, 'Keep the head of your racket above the wrist.' It is sound advice but it needs amplification.

Accepted without analysis, most people interpret this saying as 'Keep the head of the racket farther away from the ground than the wrist,' as in drawing (a) in Fig. 33.

They would consider (b) and (c) in that diagram as contravening the advice.

GROUND

Fig. 33

Factually, in terms of actual racket control, the relevant factor is the angle made by the forearm and racket handle. So long as that angle D in the drawings is less than 180°, racket control should be satisfactory. When, as in (c), the wrist drops below the line of the forearm and angle D exceeds 180°, there is significant loss of racket control.

One other object of 'keeping the racket head above the wrist' is that it entails bending the knees to get down to low returns, thus keeping the eyes and head nearer to the ball than when one bends from the hips and extends the hitting arm to compensate for straight legs. This upsets body balance alarmingly.

TIMING

Psychologists say that ball sense is developed in the first seven years of life. The more a child throws, kicks, catches, bounces and otherwise plays with a ball during those years, the more adept he will be later on. I am in no position either to dispute or to support this. Certainly it seems some young people have a natural sense of timing while others do not. The former need little or no help, the latter a great deal. Whether or not they can ever become sufficiently adept to reach championship standard is difficult to decide because there seems to be no way of measuring latent but untried talent for timing.

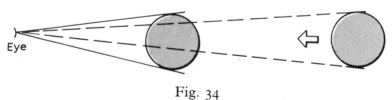

Fig. 34

So far as tennis is concerned, I would define timing as the ability to hit a moving ball with the centre of a racket face at the moment when that racket is swinging with maximum acceleration.

This involves moving to the correct hitting position and, while so doing, computing the rate of change in the ball's velocity. Thus the

48

eyes must focus quickly, adjust smoothly to the changing angle made by the boundaries of the ball as it speeds towards those eyes (see Fig. 34), and then relay the information accurately to the brain for computing so that the necessary instructions can be transmitted via the neural system to the muscles required for action. Against a service averaging 90 m.p.h. between server and receiver, all this must happen in just over half a second. Since reaction tests on motorists show two-fifths of a second to be faster than average, even the richest latent talent needs the help it can get from developed techniques.

It is as well to emphasise here that the eyes are not the only sense organs which help in assessing the pace of the ball. Sound is also important, as I found when I suddenly became stone deaf in the middle of a match many years ago. Luckily the affliction was only temporary but my first three swings after going deaf all missed the ball completely. If someone had told me this would happen I simply would not have believed him.

The reality was horribly, scarifyingly true. After those three 'air shots' I began to connect again but not until my hearing returned the next day did my timing become good again.

Eyesight deficiencies can also be overcome, as Christine Truman Jones proved by gaining a world number two ranking back in 1959. Theory shows the need for two separated eyes to draw two imaginary lines on an object in order to give it three dimensional perspective. Christine's left eye is sightless yet few women in tennis history have timed a forehand drive as well, let alone better.

So even if you do not seem like a natural timer of a moving ball, do not despair. Learn the 'language of tennis'—see 'Reading the game' later in this book—in order to understand movement and position and harness artificial aids to obtain the necessary rhythm.

Practice hitting the ball just after the top of its bounce with undeviating discipline because this involves watching the ball, carefully assessing its pace, trajectory and direction, moving smoothly into position, beginning the backswing at just the right moment and swinging the racket for impact at the specified moment in the ball's flight towards you.

Unspoken verbal instructions to oneself help, so say 'bounce', 'pause', 'hit' at the appropriate moments. Maybe trying to simulate the lilt of a waltz will help because good timing is a form of rhythm. In swinging the racket start slowly, hesitate fractionally and then let the racket flow forward into the hit with the body pivoting gracefully. Practice gently against a wall, striving all the time to feel the rhythm of ball flight and racket swing.

Once on the practice court, persuade your partner to feed you medium pace shots which impose no pressure. Again, seek rhythm and let power come in its wake. No matter how vigorously you swing your racket throughout the whole range of the stroke, it will count for little or nothing if maximum acceleration comes outside the 'zip area'—that 18–24 inches of travel immediately before and after impact.

Seek to gauge that accleration so that the racket strings appear to be chasing the ball along its flight back across the net. Seek deliberately to extend the time racket strings and ball remain in contact.

Beware of letting your timing become completely automatic for then you will suffer vulnerability to subtle changes of pace. Think about hitting the ball just after the top of its bounce and chant to yourself rhythmically 'bounce, pause, hit' in waltz time.

Practice bouncing and catching games against a wall. If there are two walls at right angles to one another, throw the ball so it hits first one, then the other, before rebounding at varying angles. Experiment with spins, kick the ball about, carry it in a pocket to play with at spare moments.

No one may know your latent talent for timing. I'll guarantee that one year of training in the ways just suggested will bring about immense improvement—and give you a great deal of harmless pleasure.

Chapter Four

Advanced Groundstrokes

Beginners normally take the racket straight back, pause, and then swing it forward again to hit the ball. This back, wait, forward and hit action applies both on the forehand and backhand.

As progress is made most players develop from this to a continuous movement in which the backswing is linked to the forward part of the swing by a loop.

There are two theories about this loop. One, which is much favoured in America, postulates that the swing back should line up with the height the player expects the ball to bounce. Thus the back and forward parts of the entire swing will be on very much the same level and the loop which links them comparatively shallow.

The other theory suggests it is advantageous to take the racket back high—'past the nose' say some coaches—so that the loop is deep, as shown by Figs. 35 and 36. There is one important advantage to a high take-back and that is when the ball hops or bounces unexpectedly high.

The racket is already moving and so it is easy to adjust the loop to the new height; the movement remains in the same direction, namely back, loop downwards and forward.

If the swing is back along the expected height of the bounce and the ball hops, the adjusting change of the swing has to be *upwards*. This is not only fundamentally unnatural, leading to a basic loss of rhythm, but also contrary to the technique that you are almost certainly learning.

So, all other things being equal, I am strongly in favour of taking the racket back high for both forehand and backhand

a   b   c

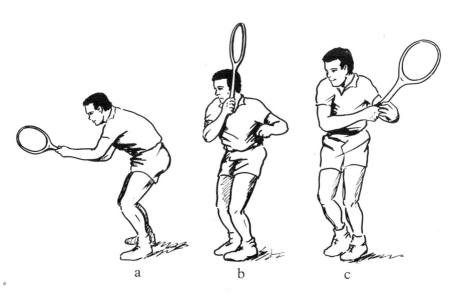

a   b   c

d   e   f

d   e   f

groundstrokes because it is easy to adjust the depth of the loop which connects the back and forward parts of the swing.

It is overwhelmingly difficult to adjust a low swing back to a surprise high bouncing ball.

Because of the comparative slowness of human reaction time relative to the speed of a fiercely driven tennis ball, there is normally insufficient time to adjust a stroke to counter an unexpected deviation in the flight of the ball, e.g. a 'shooter' off a wet patch of grass.

Therefore it is useful to have a technique which permits easy modification of the racket swing once it has begun and one of these techniques lies in a high take-back of the racket.

This is shown in Figs. 35 and 36. Fig. 35(a) and (b) and Fig. 36(a) and (b) show the position of readiness and the racket being taken back past the nose. The remaining pictures show how a linking loop joins the backswing to the forward swing and hit. The depth of that loop can be varied to cope with any return that does not bounce above head height and the adjustment is always from top to bottom. Only if the ball rears up sharply will it have to be swung higher than the position of racket in Fig. 35(b) and Fig. 36(b).

Note that the modification of the swing is not strictly a see-think-act operation but is rather a semi-reflex action, and reflexes are considerably faster than reactions.

A *Lawn Tennis* magazine study showed that high take-back players produced fewer miss-hits and miss-timings than those who take the racket straight back, pause, and then swing forward again on the same plane.

Control of the loop also simplifies application of spin—or hitting without it.

Examine Fig. 37, noticing how in the case of the flat (without spin) hit (a), the racket hand's backswing flattens at the hitting height but that in (b) the identical preparation allows the racket hand to drop below hitting height so that the strings can travel in a slightly rising plane, lifting the ball so that the top rotates forward (top spin).

Excessive spin is no longer exploited in the manner that was commonplace around the turn of the century and, later, during the

1920s, by William Tatem—'Big Bill'—Tilden, perhaps the greatest player in history.

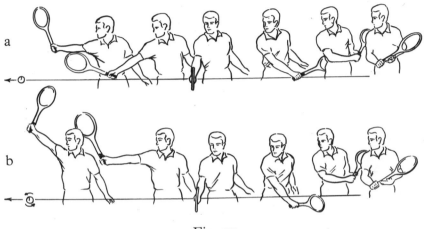

Fig. 37

Improved courts, more responsive and stable rackets and gut, and production line uniformity in the manufacture of tennis balls have reduced or even eliminated variables which added to the changing behaviour of a ball to which spin had been imparted.

Excessive spin, too, reduced the land speed of a stroke; the ball's passage through the air could be increased by the use of top spin but this caused it to travel in a curved, longer path. So the actual time taken in travelling from one end of the court—its land speed—was longer.

Enterprising players discovered this gave them more time to reach the ball when they advanced up court to a volleying position near the net. This partially explains the early development of volleying and, as in all forms of warfare, new forms of attack brought in their wake new forms of defence. Players abandoned excessive use of spin—especially underspin—when countering attacks from the net.

Today spin is regaining some of its early popularity. So far as groundstrokes are concerned, it may be divided into three types: top spin, chop, or slice, which is a mixture of under and side spin.

Whether or not the ball spins depends on the path travelled by the racket strings while they are in contact with the ball.

If the path is straight, with deviation neither up nor down nor left nor right, the ball will not be spun. Such strokes are known as flat drives. When viewed from the side, a flat forehand drive looks like Fig. 38.

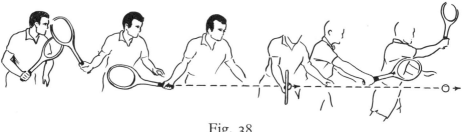

Fig. 38

In the case of the forehand lifted drive, the rising path of the strings gives the ball a slight forward rotation, as shown in Fig. 39.

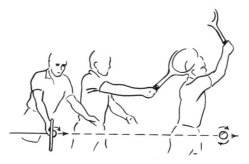

Fig. 39

To give additional top spin, it is necessary to supplement the rising plane of the racket swing with an actual upward brushing of the ball with the strings of the racket.

Remember, top spin causes the ball to dip in flight, the greater the spin, the more vicious the dip.

Under-spinning the ball with chop or slice causes the ball to rise in flight and, for a given strength of hit, increases length so that it is of most use in keeping opponents pinned to the baseline.

The amount of spin imparted for any given plane of swing or brushing of the ball is dependent on the speed at which the racket face travels. Since spin aids ball control this can cloak day to day changes in the groove of one's stroke.

Drives hit without spin are more difficult to control so that when one's swing deviates from normal, errors may rise.

Ideally one puts the swing right but in the stress of competition this is not always easy. However, a temporary improvement can often be achieved by shortening one's grip slightly, precisely by holding it half an inch or so nearer the throat than usual.

Apart from changing the actual feel of the racket, the speed at which the head travels will be diminished slightly.

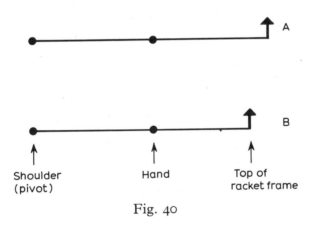

Fig. 40

Fig. 40 reveals why. If the line representing the shoulder (pivot), hand and racket face pivots through a constant arc per unit of time, everyday physics show that the tip of line B must move slightly more slowly than the tip of line A. Thus with any constant swing, there is a slight reduction in applied power in B compared with A and so less tendency for the ball to clear the base or sidelines.

However, the rate at which the racket swings is not the only factor affecting applied power. Physics tells us that force equals mass times acceleration so that if the actual speed of the swing is constant, acceleration will depend on the direction and speed in which you are running.

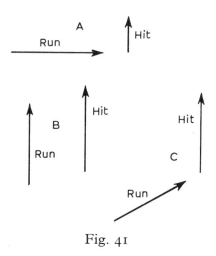

Fig. 41

Consider the factors in Fig. 41, assuming that the speed of the run is constant and representing it with the figure 1 and the speed of the racket swing with 3.

In A there is no forward run so the power applied comes only from racket swing, giving an answer 3.

In B the run is in the direction of the hit so power can be represented as 3+1 or 4, a $33\frac{1}{3}$ per cent increase over situation A.

In situation C the run is diagonally forwards at 45° from the direction of the hit. So the power will be 3+the forward force of a vector formed by the line of run and line of hit. This will be proportional to the sine of the angle, or 0·707. Thus the total power may be represented 3·707.

Clearly, compensation is vital and the practical application lies in the follow through and hit. When running fast across the baseline remember consciously to strengthen the actual hit and assist this by exaggerating the follow through.

On the other hand, when running forward, the momentum added to the drive itself may power the ball over the baseline. So compensate by applying a little top spin to the ball so that it will dip in flight.

Finally, you have been drawn up the court by a shortish return and then forced to retreat by a fast return to your feet. Your swing can still be represented by 3 but your momentum is now—1. So your total power is only 2, or half that when running forward. That conscious pressure when hitting and exaggeration of follow through is now tremendously important if your stroke is not going to put the ball in the net.

In actual play this situation occurs repeatedly when one runs into the net, is forced to back pedal to smash a lob and then quickly made to volley. In this situation I would estimate more than half the volleys end in the net because one fails to compensate for a loss of body momentum. So always after smashing aim your following volley higher over the net than usual.

FIRM BASE

Groundstrokes should be hit from a firm base for that gives the strokes stability. But a firm base does not necessarily mean a stationary one and that is a common fallacy held by many players. It is one which leads to considerable clumsiness in an alarming number of young players, to say nothing of seniors, even at advanced levels.

In order to understand this fully one must return to the physics learned in schooldays for these show that uniform movement offers equal stability to a fixed position. And, in tennis terms, this can be supplemented by smooth acceleration; has there ever been a more stable shot than the forehand drive which Fred Perry used to sweep into one or the other deep corner as he accelerated forward to crowd a short return and follow in for a winning volley.

Fig. 42 shows four curves, A representing a fixed position, B a run at uniform pace, C a run with smooth acceleration and D a dash with irregular acceleration and deceleration.

Graphically, the stability of A, B and C can be seen, as can the instability of D. Competitive players will not often allow one to hit the ball without moving (curve A). If they are experienced and at

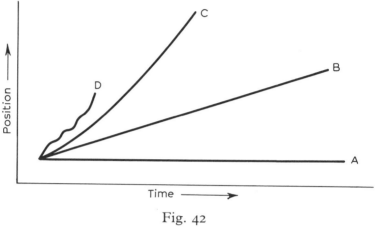

Fig. 42

all successful they won't let you run from position to position at an unvarying speed (curve B). They will force you to start and stop, twist and turn. Your object must be to move with the smoothness of curve C rather than the jerks of curve D.

This shows graphically, therefore, the relative stupidity of standing in one corner with a friend standing in, say, the opposite corner and hitting the ball diagonally to and fro. This is scarcely of any more practical value than banging the ball up and down the centre of the court.

Much better to fill an airline overnight bag with fifty or so tennis balls, putting a couple or more targets on the court and then persuading your friend to throw ball after ball so that you have to move around the court. Ensure that you maintain movement while hitting each ball and ask your friend to check you for smooth, rhythmic running and stroking. Especially ask him to check you every time you attempt to run, stop, hit, run for that breeds the ugly and unreliable 'front foot across' stroke which still plagues so many players.

Competitive tennis is a fluid game of flowing movement so develop your strokes with that in mind.

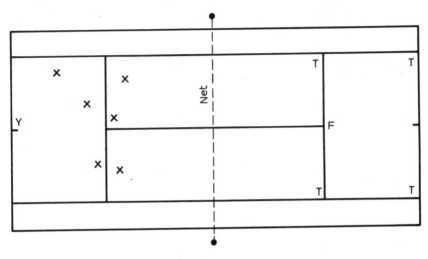

Fig. 43

Let your friend stand at position F as shown in Fig. 43 while you go to Y. Then let him throw balls in all kinds of sequences to the spots X on your side of the net. Your task is to maintain rhythmic movement while trying to hit targets at spots marked T on the diagram.

WHY WATCH THE BALL?

Modern tennis matches contain many rallies in which the ball exceeds 60 m.p.h. travelling from baseline to baseline. In terms of a court, that speed can be expressed as approximately 30 yards per second.

British School of Motoring braking reaction measurements show that the national average for seeing and acting is 0·7 seconds. They consider 0·4 seconds pretty fast. In a test against Stirling Moss racing driver Tony Brookes recorded 0·2 seconds. Probably Ken Rosewall and Rod Laver react about as quickly as Brookes but, again, 0·4 (two-fifths of a second) is almost twice as fast as average.

But in two-fifths of a second a ball travelling at 60 m.p.h. moves 12 yards, almost the full distance from net to baseline (see Fig. 44). Thus it seems that a stroke movement must be inaugurated at latest when the ball crosses the net and, because of this two-fifths of a second time barrier, it cannot be modified once the ball is 1 yard inside the receiver's court.

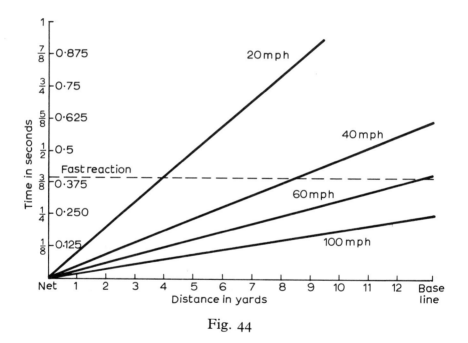

Fig. 44

So watching the ball in terms of stroke correction appears pointless, unless you are a Rosewall or Laver and react at twice that speed, so gaining 6 yards of ball travel.

Why, then, bother to try to watch the ball to impact?

The real reason is subtler. Get up and walk around in a circle. Then sit down again. Having done this, analyse the movement. Certainly control did not come from the feet. Actually it derived from the brain and was governed by the head and shoulders.

So the primary benefit on a true court where the bound of the ball is regular lies in the way watching the ball keeps the eyes down. This prevents over-anxious jerkings up of head and shoulders before impact which result in the racket swing zooming upwards and the ball flying over the far baseline. Indeed, I recall Gail Chanfreau racing up for a Maria Bueno drop shot at the Stade Roland Garros, lifting her head as she swung, and carting the ball over the stadium fence into the boulevard behind it.

So, if for no other reason, watch the ball as closely as possible in order to keep your head and shoulders steady, even if you cannot correct your swing to deal with unexpected deviations in flight of a fast ball once it has crossed the net towards you.

However, what are unexpected deviations? And are all strokes reactive? Do they not become reflex movements after ceaseless practice?

Reflex actions do not go through the sense—transmit to brain—decision—tell muscles—action cycle. The sense—action link takes place in the spinal cord, the resultant time saving becoming immense.

Anyone who has seen Ken Rosewall volley 100 m.p.h. smashes when only 6 yards or so away from the hit must realise that he could not possibly have reacted in one-eighth of a second and even reflexes would have been severely tested to see a ball and move a racket into position so rapidly.

The answer, of course, is that continuous, intelligent stroke practice has been allied to a highly developed ability to 'read' the game as a whole, making him one of the fastest players in history.

Rosewall shows that, on an uneven court, the stroke is begun but the mind is aware of the possibility of a 'shooter' or 'kicker' and the racket is controlled accordingly. Consequently, the late part of the swing can be modified in far less time than the faster than average two-fifths of a second which may be assumed as the norm for international class players.

By all means watch the ball for the benefits listed above but in considering improved stroke technique, change to the dynamic tenet, 'hit the ball just after the top of the bounce'. This involves watching the ball, but as a means to action necessitating judgment of pace, length and direction of ball flight and movement to cope with all of these. Just try doing this without watching the ball and keeping your head down.

As basic approach, then, adopt the 'hit the ball just after the top of the bounce' system and start right away to develop your ability to read the opponent's intentions even before he hits the ball. It can be done.

However, like all advice, this is not absolute. There are times when it must be disregarded, so it must remain your servant and never become your master.

The two most important situations are (1) when an opportunity to attack arises and (2) when one is attacked from the net oneself.

Remember, a tennis net is 3 feet high at the centre band. Waist high on the average man is 3 inches lower than this and a ball struck just after the top of its bounce is likely to be 3 inches lower than that. So to go over the net, the ball must travel a rising path until it clears the net; only then should it start descending.

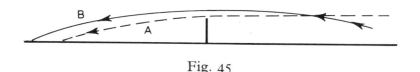

Fig. 45

Compare line A with line B in Fig. 45. The former represents a drive hit at shoulder height by a man 6 feet tall from a position on his own service line. The ball needs little spin or pull of gravity to remain in court but can achieve the near physical impossibility of travelling in almost a straight line and still land within the opponent's baseline.

Line B depicts a ball hit just below waist level by the same man. It has to be lifted to clear the net and so must either be reduced in speed or given top spin or a mixture of both. Relative to A, pace and angle are considerably restricted.

The practical problem besetting the man who conscientiously hits the ball just after the top of the bounce in normal rally play is in maintaining the concentration and mental drive to spot quickly any return which should be attacked and then to produce the change of attitude which sparks a sudden pounce forward to force the ball as it is rising or at the top of its bounce.

This is far more a mental problem than one of technique. It necessitates considerable determination. That determination can be developed through consistent mental rehearsal. Fifteen minutes of this each day will condition the subconscious to action, or so believers in psychocybernetics avow.

Similarly, when being attacked by an approach shot which is followed to the net, the alert man who is seeking positively to advance his game will deliberately move forward to take the ball higher in its post-bounce flight. Apart from the increased angles this added height offers, each yard forward the defender can move equals 2 yards in flight time, i.e. the distance saved in the ball coming to his racket and going back across the net. Against an approach shot struck from the opponent's service line, 1 yard equals

$\dfrac{1}{13+7}$ yards or 5 per cent.

So take as basic 'hit the ball just after the top of its bounce,' but be ever zealous for the moments when it is better to move a step or two forward in order to hit it at a higher point in its post-bounce trajectory.

FOREHAND CHECK POINTS

(a) Ball going too high or over baseline

(1) Head and shoulders jerking up too soon, perhaps because of anxiety to see where ball is going.
(2) Letting the racket face tilt back at moment of impact.
(3) Hitting the ball behind the correct point of impact.

(4) Letting the ball drop too low and not bending knees.

(5) Letting body weight fall backwards while making the stroke.

(6) Snatching racket head upwards in following through instead of letting racket and shoulder continue in a continuous, smooth flow after striking ball.

(7) Slapping the ball with excessive wrist action instead of keeping wrist firm.

(8) Rushing straight at ball instead of lightly skipping to its side.

(9) Incorrect grip. Hand too much on top of handle.

(b) Ball going into net

(1) Aiming too near the top of the net.

(2) Letting the racket face tilt forward—'choke'—before impact for fear of hitting out. A common fault when nervous.

(3) Restricting the follow through.

(4) Hitting the ball in front of correct point of impact.

(5) Failing to compensate for loss of body weight when running at right angles.(straight across court) to the line you wish to hit the ball along. Exaggerate the follow through to prevent this.

(6) Letting the ball drop too low and then not bending knees to permit your racket to lift it upwards over net.

(7) Whipping the ball with a wrist action instead of letting arm and shoulder swing the racket.

(8) Letting front leg step too far across and so choke the swing.

(9) Rushing and getting too near the ball.

(10) Trying for too much top spin.

(11) Incorrect grip. Hand too far behind the back of the handle.

(12) Failing to make the racket face chase the ball after impact as though trying to hold it on the strings.

(13) Front shoulder dipping down.

(c) Ball going to the left

(1) Facing the ball and failing to pivot.

(2) Hitting in front of correct point of impact.

(3) Bending wrist to left so ball is hit with a hook.
(4) Swinging body and arm into shot too soon.
(5) Checking the upper part of arm and completing swing by bending lower arm at elbow.
(6) Taking racket back too far to right, so moving the racket head diagonally forwards from right to left when hitting.
(7) Hitting ball too near to body.

(d) Ball going to the right

(1) Tilting the racket face backwards when hitting the ball.
(2) Pulling body weight backwards when making stroke.
(3) Dropping racket head and opening racket face to the right when hitting.
(4) Hitting the ball behind the correct point of impact.
(5) Hitting the ball too near the body.
(6) Snatching the racket follow through upwards instead of letting it swing through smoothly.
(7) Lifting the head and slicing the ball. (See section on spin.)
(8) Failing to pivot body into the stroke after turning into sideways position.

BACKHAND CHECK POINTS

(a) Ball going into net

(1) Aiming too near to the top of the net.
(2) Hitting the ball too far in front of the correct point of impact.
(3) Turning the racket face over the top of the ball at impact.
(4) Failing to bend knees in order to let racket travel in an upward plane before, at, and after the point of impact.
(5) Hitting the ball too near the body.
(6) Hitting the ball with body facing the net.
(7) Restricting backswing and so losing power.
(8) Failing to swing the racket forward in a slightly rising plane.
(9) Rushing at the ball instead of skipping lightly into a position

in which it can be hit just after the top of its bounce.

(10) Not supporting racket with left hand during the backswing.

(11) Thumb around handle instead of diagonally across it.

(b) Ball going over baseline

(1) Head and shoulders jerking up before moment of impact to see opponent's court position.

(2) Racket head falling below wrist during forward swing.

(3) Failing to bend knees and tilting the racket face upwards to compensate.

(4) Body weight falling backwards while hitting the ball.

(5) Exaggerating the follow through in an upward direction.

(6) Arm bending and elbow leading swing.

(7) Weak wrist and grip setting up an unconscious slice under the ball during impact.

(8) Body square to net instead of sideways.

(c) Ball going to the right

(1) Body square to the net when making shot.

(2) Restricted backswing causing the follow through to be forced.

(3) Swinging into the shot too soon so that ball is struck forward of the correct point of impact.

(4) Bending wrist so racket face inclines to the right.

(5) Pulling racket with forehand grip instead of rotating it slightly so that fleshy part of thumb is slightly behind handle.

(6) Not adjusting timing to a slightly slower return by the opponent. Never let timing become unthinkingly automatic. Always judge the oncoming ball's pace and adjust timing accordingly.

(d) Ball going to the left

(1) Grip or wrist too weak, thus failing to resist the power of the oncoming ball.

(2) Slowness in beginning the backswing and so hitting ball

behind the correct point of impact.

(3) Failing to get out of path of ball and so pushing it away from body instead of hitting it from the side.

(4) Letting wrist bend backwards when swinging forward.

behind the correct point of impact.
(3) Failing to get out of path of ball and so pushing it away from body instead of hitting it from the side.
(4) Letting wrist bend backwards when swinging forward.

Chapter Five

Net Play and Defence Against It

When Spencer W. Gore won the inaugural Wimbledon singles back in 1877 the net was $4\frac{3}{4}$ feet at the posts and 4 feet at the centre. Today it is $3\frac{1}{2}$ feet at the posts. Imagine how much harder a ball may now be hit down the line and still not fly over the baseline, than in Gore's day when it had to soar $33\frac{1}{3}$ per cent higher half-way through its flight.

Gore realised this immediately so in his matches he constantly advanced to the net to volley the ball at an angle quite beyond his opponent's reach. Because there was little danger of a ball travelling fast enough to pass him down the line, he advanced very near to the net—so near that his racket was frequently over the net on his opponent's side when he hit the ball.

The rules for 1878 prohibited this and a wily opponent realised he could not speed shots laterally beyond Gore's reach at the net. Instead, he tossed the ball high over Gore's head; the lob was invented and the battle between volley and groundstroke specialists, which has gone on for almost a hundred years, was well and truly begun.

Ignoring tactics and considering only court geometry, the nearer one is to the net when hitting the ball, the greater are the angles which can be exploited. Fig. 46 shows this graphically. O and O represent parts of the court to which the ball may reasonably be hit, whether from the baseline or near the net.

The angle from the volleying position V is twice that from position GS. Hence the likelihood of placing the ball out of reach is immeasurably greater from V than from GS.

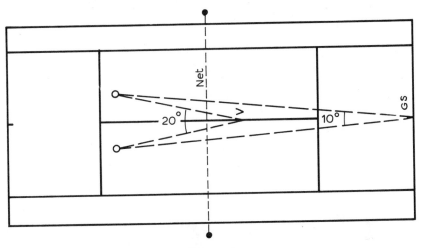

Fig. 46

Footwork, balance, flexible knees, neck and hips, racket head above the wrist, eyes on the ball, a strong forward movement and correct facing of the racket are all vital factors in the forehand volley. Above all, flexible knees, which significantly help all the other factors.

In Fig. 47, the correct use of these factors is shown in the 'right' series of pictures. Note particularly that by deep bending of the knees the centre of balance is central to the whole body and well down, so that the body is kept virtually perpendicular, the racket head above wrist level, and the eyes close to the ball. The forward movement and follow through of the racket thrust are both in an upwards direction, so ensuring the ball clears the net.

In the 'wrong' sequence the volleyer's knees are stiff and he has to drop the racket head well below wrist level to connect with the ball. Thus his eyes and the contact point are 60 per cent farther apart than when the knees are bent. If the volleyer tries to compensate for this with a deeper bend he sets up serious imbalance and puts an unnecessary strain on the back—and there is also a lateral loss of balance as picture three shows.

The same factors show when the backhand volley is made correctly

71

right

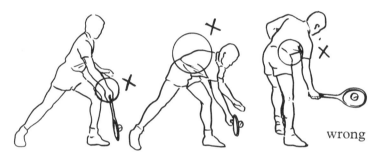

wrong

Fig. 47

and incorrectly (Fig. 48). Straight knees cause strain, loss of balance and a dropped racket head. So to improve your low volleying undertake exercises which increase the flexibility of your knees.

Volley power dominates modern tennis, punching home openings forced by services and groundstrokes.

Volleys are punched before the ball has bounced and 30 feet or more forward of your baseline position so milliseconds are decisive.

Fig. 49(a) shows mental and physical alertness, ready-to-spring poise and, especially, the racket already up, not down, eager for instant action.

Fig. 49(b). It's a forehand. Eyes intently focus the ball, left arm helps balance and the racket head is positioned to punch at and through the ball. There is virtually no backswing.

72

right

wrong

Fig. 48

Fig. 49(c). Forceful fighters step forward when they punch and so do aggressive volleyers. The wrist is locked, the grip firm and thrust is added from the upper arm and shoulder.

73

Fig. 49(d) emphasises the thrusting action. In groundstrokes the feel is of swinging and the ball must be lifted to clear the net. Most volleys are punched above net level so the ball can be angled firmly downwards beyond the opponent's reach. The head and eyes are nearer to the ball than when hitting groundstrokes.

a   b   c   d   e

Fig. 49

Fig. 49(e). Jabbing punches have little follow through, nor have punching volleys. The racket head travels along the line the ball was punched . . . and the eyes remain focused on it. Leg and arm are used to maintain balance in case of quick returns.

In top class, 100 m.p.h. tennis, volley follows volley in tenths of seconds. It's fast and it's fun.

Unnecessary fear ruins many backhand volleys. The secrets of success are intense concentration, early preparation, a firm grip with thumb behind the handle, locked wrists, firm lower and upper arm and shoulder and a solid, punching movement.

Fig. 50(a). The volleyer moves towards the backhand, eyes glued on ball, racket up in readiness for instant action and supported by the left hand.

Fig. 50(b). He is moving towards the ball, racket back—but not too far—in readiness to punch straight through the ball. The left

a　　　b　　　c　　　d

Fig. 50

hand is still supporting the racket. Right shoulder pointed at oncoming ball.

Fig. 50(c). The moment of impact. Weight forward, eyes on ball, racket head well up with braced wrist, thumb behind handle for extra thrust and the racket just released from supporting, punch-adding left hand. Knees bent.

Fig. 50(d). The short, thrusting follow-through with eyes still on ball and left hand aiding balance. The racket head has 'chased' the ball in order to emphasise the punching jab through it.

If you reach a forward position in court behind an aggressive approach shot you normally hold superiority. Volley the return weakly and you immediately revert to a position of inferiority; you are isolated, with yards of space between you and each sideline and your opponent is only a dozen or so yards away. The ball is convenient for him to blast a passing shot into whichever gap he chooses.

Remember always, then, that the object of any volley should be to end the rally immediately. This will not be possible every time but still think positively of putting your opponent in as difficult a court position as possible.

To this end, the majority—80 per cent or even more—of your volleys should be deep, within 4 feet or even less of the baseline. Most players volley for the gap in the opponent's court. That's fine providing he or she cannot reach the ball. However, most players run and stroke more easily in covering a gap than when they are forced to turn.

So do not be afraid of volleying the ball deep back to the spot from which it has just been hit. This is especially valid on your opponent's backhand wing.

Most men of tournament standard make use of serve and run into volley tactics. This particular sequence is normally most effective when serving in the backhand court, as illustrated in Fig. 51.

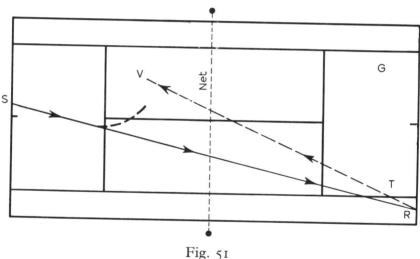

Fig. 51

S serves to R's backhand and runs in. R returns across court (broken line) to V. S, running along the line of the ball, swerves towards V and has the choice of volleying either for the gap G or to make R, who should be covering the gap, turn and play the ball at T.

If the return is high and the chances high of volleying the ball out of reach, aim for G. If in doubt, especially on key points, volley for T and close in with the intention of finishing the point with the following volley or smash if lobbed.

This leads on to the way in which volleying should be practised. Almost always when watching a coaching session one sees the teacher hitting the ball to the pupil and the pupil volleying the ball back so that the master can again hit it to him. . . . And so the 'rally' continues.

Frequently the master and pupil stand just forward of their respective service lines and volley the ball back and forth. It looks effective and, considered unthinkingly, seems an effective form of practice. But is it?

From *Tennis: How to Become a Champion* you can learn the physiological facts of grooving. In one sentence, every time you make or even think a particular action, the easier it becomes to repeat it next time.

So, if you practise volleying a ball to a person you will be grooving neuro-patterns that will tend always to make you volley to him—and the object of volleying is to place the ball beyond his reach. So have 30 seconds or a minute of volleying to and fro to get your eye in but then change to volleying out of the other person's reach. It may be tiresome having to stop to collect the balls every minute or so but that is better than grooving bad habits into your nervous system.

There is a lively, enjoyable game which provides good volleying practice. It is called 'goals'.

In the way schoolboys roll up their coats to use them as 'goal posts' for football in the playground or park, use four old boxes or something similar to make goals on each of the two service lines. How far in from each sideline depends on age, size and proficiency but a couple of feet in either side will do for a start. Fig. 52 shows the players, A and B, at the moment of service. A starts by hitting a ball between the 'posts' of his goal to his opponent, B, standing on his goal line. From then on the object is to volley the ball between the posts for a goal. After service and return of service each player may move where he wishes; as in normal tennis, the best direction is forward, so as to narrow the opponent's angle and to reduce the length of time he has to reach the volley. A and B serve alternatively, changing after each rally.

77

This game increases speed, improves ability to place the ball, and is good fun to play. A 'match' can be of five minutes duration, first to score five goals, and so on. Only volleys score, even if your volley directs the ball on to the ground before it goes between the 'goal posts'.

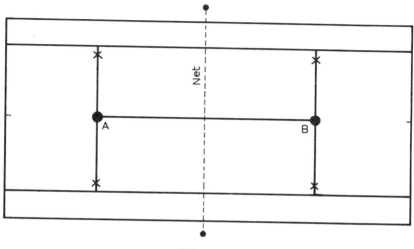

Fig. 52

Such volleying practice speeds up movement and reflexes tremendously, an important factor because accurate footwork is even more important in volleying than it is in hitting groundshots.

Remember, the feel of a volley should be one of punching the ball. As in boxing, a punch carries extra power when the body weight thrusts forward in unison. So the most forceful volleys are usually struck by stepping forward into the shot, the front leg taking all the weight at the moment of impact.

However, when two—or four, as in doubles—men are slamming a ball at one another from about 4 yards range there frequently isn't time to move the feet. This need not prevent use of the hips to bring body pivot into the stroke. The time really is very limited; 60 m.p.h., a slowish ball speed for volleys, means only two-fifths of a second between volley and volley at 4 yards range.

In a normal reaction and reaction operation the eye sees the ball and transmits details to the brain which sends electrical messages speeding to the muscles needed for action via the nervous system. Two-fifths of a second is a fast reaction; this includes the passage of the 'orders' via the nerves—at roughly 30 yards per second according to D. Stark Murray, BSc, MB, ChB.

So there is no time to waste—not even a couple of milliseconds.

Fortunately experience, intelligent coaching and purposeful practice enable a dedicated player to 'read' what is happening faster than the normal action-reaction time and this is explained later on in this book.

Racket hold plays an important part in successful volleying at speed. At least 80 per cent of players, even of Wimbledon standard, hold the racket too low and too close to the body so that before they can punch it into a ball speeding towards them at shoulder level, they first have to bring the racket up to that level. Only then can they punch it forward. Remembering that typical two-fifths of a second they have for action, can they really afford the relaxing luxury of letting the racket droop low?

How you hold your racket depends ultimately on your personal ideas of comfort—but, remember, something which may at first seem uncomfortable may well become comfortable through very little practice and be significantly advantageous technically.

So try, even if you soon abandon it, holding your racket with the backhand grip out in front of your left shoulder with the left hand supporting it at its throat. Let the arms be midway between straight out in front and full bend.

Try this on a court by having a friend hit balls more or less straight at you from the baseline. Face the net and adjust your position by moving the appropriate foot left or right.

Hold the racket tightly, keep your wrist firm, put the racket face in front of the oncoming ball and thrust it firmly forwards. With this racket position even the fastest returns can be met by the strings and if the forward thrust is slight, the speed of the oncoming ball will bounce it back effectively.

This system helps the confidence of players fearful of being hit by the ball. As their confidence grows, so they become quick and proficient in slipping the hand and racket into position for forehand volleys.

LOBS AND DINKS

A tennis ball hit in an upward direction has several forces acting on it: (a) gravity, which with time decreases the upward power of the hit, (b) the basic resistance of the air through which it is travelling allied to the air resistance offered by the nap of the cover—or lack of it, and (c) spin.

This can be expressed in terms well known in gunnery, namely the equation of the descending parabola: $y = ax^2 + bx + c$.

Giving a, b and c arbitary values of $-\frac{1}{4}$, $\frac{3}{2}$ and o, it is possible to plot the path of the ball over the length of court.

x	$\frac{3x}{2}$	x^2	$\frac{x^2}{4}$	$\frac{3x}{2} - \frac{x^2}{4}$	Each unit of x = 13 feet. $\therefore$ x13
0	0	0	0	0	0
1	$1\frac{1}{2}$	1	$\frac{1}{4}$	$1\frac{1}{4}$	$16\frac{1}{4}$
2	3	4	1	2	26
3	$4\frac{1}{2}$	9	$2\frac{1}{4}$	$2\frac{1}{4}$	$30\frac{1}{4}$
4	6	16	4	2	26
5	$7\frac{1}{2}$	25	$6\frac{1}{4}$	$1\frac{1}{4}$	$16\frac{1}{4}$
6	9	36	9	0	0

To keep the numbers comfortable, each value of x represents 13 feet of court. The path of the ball can now be plotted. It works out as in Fig. 53.

To convert this theory, which has existed since the time of Descartes, into something of practical value for tennis players, pause to think for a moment. Look again at the plot of the ball. The figures have assumed no wind and it ascends and descends in curves that mirror each other.

Therefore, when lobbing from on or just inside the baseline forget the man at the net or running in to volley. Instead, hit the ball in an upwards arc, judging your strength so it reaches the top of the arc directly above the net.

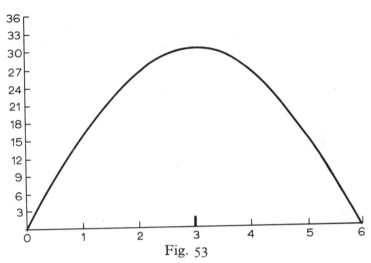

Fig. 53

It doesn't matter whether you hit a high or low lob, simply forget everything except the net and making it the high spot of your hit. The basic laws of physics will ensure that it comes down to earth at the same distance from the baseline as your own position in court.

Once you become adept at judging the power to use, you can adjust to compensate when you are more than, say, 5 feet inside your own baseline. If you are 6 feet inside and wish to lob on the opposite baseline, judge the high spot of the lob to be 3 feet beyond the net.

The great advantage of this system is that the net, unlike your opponent, never moves. It is always 39 feet nearer to you than your opponent's baseline. So instead of thinking about or trying to keep half an eye on him, you simply concentrate on the net.

The same kind of thinking can be applied to passing shots. Your opponent is constantly moving, his sidelines are not. If you try to evade him you are exposing yourself to dangers of erring. Concentrate on the lines, make them your targets, and try to out-think him when choosing one or the other as your target. He will out-guess you occasionally but less frequently than you will err through watching him rather than the ball. And even when he guesses right, he still has to hit a winning volley.

To that end, I am inclined to recommend 'when in doubt, dink'. There is nothing more difficult than making a winning volley off a 'nothing' ball which droops at half pace, low across the net and at an angle which runs the ball away from your racket. These 'dinks' will be doubly effective once you have mastered the descending parabola theory of lobbing and so can either toss the ball over his head or droop on his toes at will. He will never know when to close right in for the dink or hang back for the lob and that will shatter his confidence. And successful volleyers must be confident.

Success with these methods demands good ball control so perhaps now is the moment to read once more the factors which make for ball control (page 23).

There are two categories of lobs, straight and diagonal. Both have advantages and disadvantages. Take diagonals first. Recalling Pythagoras, the square on the hypotenuse is equal to the sum of the squares on the other two sides of a right angled triangle.

A tennis court (singles) is 78 feet long and 27 feet wide. The diagonal, therefore, is $\sqrt{78^2+27^2}$, or just over 82 feet. So when lobbing from one corner to another you have around 4 extra feet to play with compared with a straight lob. That's quite a lot of extra court.

However, the ball will take longer to travel 82 feet than it will 78 feet so your opponent will have a fraction extra of time to chase back and retrieve the ball. He is also likelier to be more adept at smashing diagonal lobs, specially those from backhand to backhand, because most people lob that way and he will be well practised.

On the other hand, a lob from the backhand corner straight down his forehand line will repeatedly win points simply because players are unused to running backwards from the middle of the court to the junction of the baseline and forehand sideline.

It is always dangerous to generalise but when in doubt and on the defensive, lob diagonally BUT be sure to give the ball considerable height and be long rather than short. Nothing helps a volleyer's confidence more than a few short lobs which he can kill easily. So rather than nurture his confidence, lob deep, even at the risk of the ball clearing the baseline. If it does, well, at least you have robbed him of smashing practice and that may just help to make him miss when you do happen to send him a short lob.

Chapter 6 shows how top spin and back spin or slice affect the flight of the ball. Top spin tends to keep the ball nearer to the parabolic path (a) of Fig. 54. Thus it is used for low trajectory, aggressive lobs aimed just to clear the net man's racket and then run away from him rapidly after bouncing.

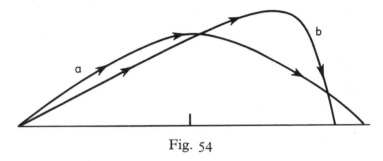

Fig. 54

Backspin and, to a lesser degree, slice sharpen the angle of descent; indeed, a high, deep lob hit with backspin (b) brings the ball down almost straight (perpendicular to the ground). If they are really high and come down within 3 feet or less of the baseline, such lobs are difficult to kill outright.

THE SMASH

The telling answer to a good lob is an even better smash. That is a stroke somewhat akin to the service but with someone else governing the throw-up and sending the ball very much higher. To compensate for the increased difficulties in timing, the swing has to be shortened.

Fig. 55 depicts good style in this vital stroke. The man at the net, alert, has 'picked' the lob quickly and is backing down his half of the court in sideways, chassé steps like a refugee from television's 'Come Dancing'.

Fig. 55

His eyes remain focused on the ball, his racket drops behind his right shoulder and his left hand points at the ball.

This is a first class way of keeping the ball in view and an excellent way of developing your smash or of putting it right when it goes wrong is to practice catching the ball as in the third picture of the series.

Determine that whenever the opponent lobs the point will be yours. Banish half-heartedness, jump, as in picture four, to obtain added height, glue your eyes on the ball and keep that left arm pointing upwards. There is no better way of combatting the natural tendency to drop the head too soon, thus maximising the chances of poor timing or even missing the ball altogether.

Go for depth when the lob is deep. When the lob is short, smash the ball downward at an angle which bounces it into the side netting surrounding the court.

Lobs vary in height and trajectory. In Fig. 56, line A represents a low, aggressive lob hit with slight top spin. The ball makes a comparatively narrow angle with line X, which represents the forward movement of the racket.

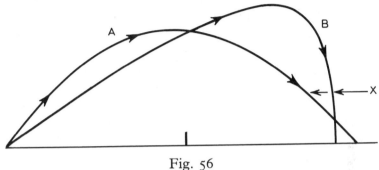

Fig. 56

Compare this angle with the one between X and line B, which represents a high, defensive lob hit with backspin. That spin and the pull of gravity have caused the ball to descend almost perpendicularly; if it is a really high lob 'g' will cause the ball to drop very fast. The time for contact between ball and centre of racket face is minute relative to path A.

Therefore the racket must also move fast. So high lobs must be dealt with confidently and powerfully.

It is tempting to let the ball bounce but I cannot advocate this to any ambitious player. Confidence is a strange personality factor. The more one shows it, the more it grows. Conversely, the more one becomes cautious, even though caution may be the intellectually correct course, the more caution will permeate one's entire attitude, on and off a tennis court. And in tennis, whether played as a career or for pure pleasure, caution is not a very valuable ally.

Most opponents lob diagonally to one's backhand corner and, with practice, one soon becomes proficient in backing in that direction and smashing from above the left shoulder.

I recall telling Patti Hogan to lob that great Australian player Margaret Court to the forehand corner. Mrs Court was so unaccustomed to moving backwards from court centre to her own forehand corner that she actually hit one smash full pitch over the back canvas of the court and Patti pulled off one of the major surprises of that year in winning.

Good tactics are seldom based on obvious ideas; surprise is their essence.

To summarise, effective smashing of lobs demands rapid and sure footwork, careful watching of the ball (helped by pointing at the ball with the left hand), a shortened service swing, absence of spin when hitting, and determination to end the rally once and for all. Develop these attributes and confidence will quickly increase. That increase will bring increased proficiency—more confidence will follow—and so proceed ad infinitum.

Chapter Six

Refinements of Play

SPIN

Though spin is seldom used today in the deliberate way it was in the early 1900s and immediately after the First World War, most tournament players use spin to a greater or lesser degree.

Spin, so far as groundstrokes are concerned, may be divided into three types, top spin, chop or under spin, and slice.

Top Spin

Top spin makes the top of the ball revolve longitudinally in the same direction as its line of flight (see Fig. 57).

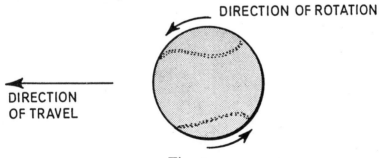

DIRECTION OF ROTATION

DIRECTION
OF TRAVEL

Fig. 57

Providing there is a little nap on the ball, the rotation of the ball will increase wind resistance at its top, reduce it at its bottom. Following the line of least resistance, the ball will dip in flight.

When the ball pitches, however, the rotation lessens ground resistance, so causing the ball to bound high and forward.

Top spin can be applied heavily by brushing the racket strings up and over the ball. It can be applied less heavily by lifting the ball slightly, the racket turning slightly over during its travel (see Fig. 58).

Fig. 58

Fig. 58 shows the slight lift and turn of the racket face during a 'lifted' drive. This is why lift and top spin are often interchanged in use.

Chop or Under Spin

Chop or under spin is the reverse of top spin, the ball being struck from top to bottom and rotated longitudinally so that the bottom of the ball rotates towards the line of flight (see Fig. 59).

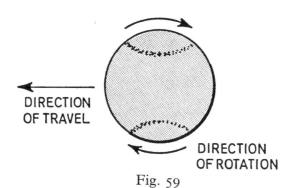

Fig. 59

Chop or under spin increases wind resistance to the bottom of the ball, reduces it at the top. The ball, following the line of least resistance, rises in its flight. But when it pitches the rotation increases ground resistance and so the ball tends to skid through low and hold back.

Slice

Slice is a mixture of chop, which causes a longitudinal backwards rotation, and of side spin (see Fig. 60).

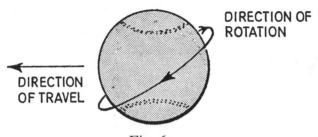

Fig. 60

The tendency of the ball is to rise in the air, and to keep low when it bounces. Whether its rise exceeds that of a chop or its bound remains lower depends on a variety of factors including the surface of the court, the nap on the ball, and the confidence of the striker. Generally, the chop is executed more purposefully, powerfully and confidently than the slice, so the ball travels more directly and lies well down after pitching. A tentative safety-first slice floats the ball through the air and lifts it after pitching. It is easy meat to any agile and ambitious volleyer.

There are, in play, two types of slice, one tentative where the racket digs at the ball and scoops it up, the other where the racket, though it imparts slice, travels very firmly and definitely straight through the point in the air where it makes contact with the ball.

In back court rally play this can be a very aggressive stroke, but it remains less useful than top spin for evading or embarrassing an opponent who volleys strongly and continually.

At park, club or even minor county levels of tennis, spin can be devastatingly effective. In top class play this is less so, for spin can only be applied at the expense of speed and speed allied to placement is the main weapon of practically every champion.

Perhaps speed should be defined in this context: it means the time a ball takes to travel from the racket to the target spot on the opponent's court.

Now use of top spin allows the ball to be hit at a terrific speed through the air, but since top spin makes the ball dip violently, it has to be given a far higher trajectory drive than a flat drive when the target is beyond the service line.

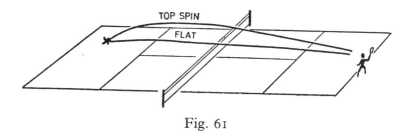

Fig. 61

Fig. 61 shows the relative paths of a flat drive and a top spin drive from the racket head to a point X in the backhand corner. The top spin drive clearly sends the ball on a much longer path and will need to be hit very much harder than the flat shot if it is to take a shorter time to reach X.

With chop or slice the effect is even worse, for the spin makes the ball rise during flight and so it must be hit softer if it is not to go beyond the target spot.

Fig. 62 shows how two shots hit at a similar height with a similar speed, one with slice or chop, the other without spin (flat) will cause the ball to travel through the air.

There is one situation in which top spin is extremely valuable and that is when the opponent is attacking near the net. Then a heavily spun, speedy shot will dip viciously beyond his racket—or force him to volley upwards and defensively—if he reaches the ball. The main loss of speed relative to the ground will not matter because it will occur after the ball has passed the volleyer; the ball will still be travelling too quickly for him to turn, chase and catch it up.

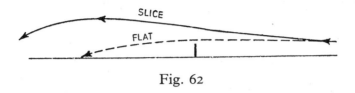

Fig. 62

In addition, the shorter ground distance—not air distance—between the hit and pitch of a top spin drive relative to a flat drive enables the striker to use far acuter angles.

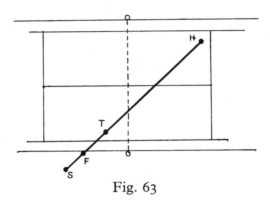

Fig. 63

Fig. 63 shows the relative air flight of three balls hit from point H with the same strength, one with top spin, another flat, the third with slice. The dip caused by top spin will cause the ball to pitch at point T while the flat shot will not pitch till F—outside the court. S pitches even farther out.

This is valuable both defensively when meeting a volleyer and offensively when forcing an opponent well beyond the sideline prior to a deep drive to the opposite corner.

This technique has been exploited particularly well be Rod Laver and Manuel Santana in men's and Darlene Hard and Lesley Turner in women's tennis.

However, it can be seen that spin is used here in a positional or manoeuvring sense. Providing he can reach the ball in fair comfort, the spin itself will scarcely embarrass the opponent.

This is not so in lower grades of tennis. I have yet to meet the ordinary park player who is not worried by chop, while top spin can, and frequently does, force average players to hit so carefully that all sting goes from their games.

An additional use of top spin is control, an important factor in those grades of tennis where new balls are scarce. At Wimbledon, where the balls are changed after the 7th, 16th, 25th, 34th and so on games, there is scarcely time for the nap to be destroyed. But a few sets on a public asphalt court reduce even the finest ball to marble smoothness and, with wind resistance so reduced, top spin is essential if the ball is not to fly.

It is also useful on courts where the baseline is near the backstop; I well recall as an inexperienced junior being completely baffled by a man who hit a succession of heavily topped, semi-lobs which pitched near the baseline and had me spending most of the morning entangled in the all too near stop netting.

Such shots must be countered when the ball is rising but it requires quite a high standard of skill to take the ball consistently on the rise and move it around the court enough to create openings or break up the opponent.

But be reminded that in top class play spin is very subservient to speed and accuracy. Not since 1930, when Tilden last won, has a Wimbledon singles champion profited from extensive and deliberate use of intentional spin.

Not that the current champions hit the ball completely flat. All use spin to some degree, that degree being the point where the speed of the flat drive is given just that modicum of lift—'lift' is the modern word for slight top spin—to keep the ball under commercial control. Perhaps Pancho Segura, whom many readers will have seen either live or on television, is the finest exemplar of the lifted forehand drive even though he uses both hands to make the shot.

For winning tennis, then, at park or club level do not be afraid to experiment with spin as a means of forcing errors from the opponent. At higher levels keep spin very much in its place as a servant to be used for opening up the opponent's court or beating a volleyer. Remember, too, that the best ground shots in the world are only about 60 per cent effective in top class play. They must be supported by equally good serving accuracy and power and naturally aggressive, enterprising and punishing volleying before they can take a man to the top.

Beware of slicing off the backhand. It is such an easy shot to develop and, once developed, is as difficult to cure as dope addiction. And a sliced backhand is the easiest target in the world for an adequate and nimble volleyer.

On the forehand the easy habit to acquire is top spin. This is far less dangerous than slice on the backhand.

Unless a player has a very fixed and reasonable determination to reach the very highest levels, he would be ill advised to allow a friend or coach to persuade him to change. Since Vic Seixas, who won Wimbledon in 1953, used excessive top spin on nearly every fore-hand, I am almost inclined to say never change a strong forehand which uses top spin for a flatter drive simply to be more orthodox. Certainly weigh the pros and cons very carefully, indeed a dozen times over—and then another dozen. But beware of changes.

READING THE GAME

Before continuing with this important chapter please equip your-self with paper and pen or pencil. Please do it now.

Now: KEN ROSEWALL HAS NEVER WON THE WIMBLEDON SINGLES.

Re-read that sentence and then write down how many times each letter appears, e.g. R crops up twice.

Put this book down and do not pick it up again until you have listed from memory how often K, R etc. occur. If you wish, write down the sentence from memory in order to count.

Stop reading until you have counted.

Right, you have finished and with little difficulty have counted a total of 41 letters, broken down as follows: K1; E7; N5; R2; O3; S4; W3; A2; L4; H2; I2; V, T, M, B, D, G 1 each=6. Total 41.

Now read the next sequence twice and then go through the same procedure: L, T, R, W, B, D, E, S, I, M, L.

There are less than one-third the total of letters in the first sequence but it is extremely doubtful if you will be able to list more than 75 per cent, and then only with intense concentration.

The reason is crystal clear. The 41 letters in the first sequence were so arranged in groups and spaces that they conformed to a system which education plus experience and practice has taught you to understand. You did not read the individual letters. Instead, you took in the message as a whole and acted on that, as distinct from the 11-letter sequence which made no understandable message or pattern. Later, it was simple to put together the 41 separate units of the message.

This theory is equally applicable to tennis. Probably you began playing with a parent, friend or coach, or all in turn. First, you learnt the game's individual 'alphabet'. Then practice and participation in matches and tournaments developed a knowledge of 'grammar', followed by a 'vocabulary'. From then on it became a matter of study, application, and experience to gain complete command of tennis 'language'. If you have reached Wimbledon standard you comprehend all that is happening in one quick glance.

Experiments by *Lawn Tennis* magazine show that full understanding can be gained from a glance of only one-sixth of a second duration.

This theory accounts for the fact that Alan Davidson, one of the greatest Australian Test Match cricketers of the post-World War II era, became good enough to gain selection for New South Wales (something akin in standard to acceptance for the British Hard Courts Singles Championship) although he had never played 'Bournemouth' class cricket and, indeed, had only ever seen it played live three times.

Davidson learned the 'language' of cricket through intense study of films, pictures and books—so intense that he was quickly able to adapt to the actuality of participating in top class play.

This is a clue to how some top line players outside Britain—inside too—have graduated from areas where facilities are abysmal compared with, say, London or Los Angeles. If motivation, intelligence, application, and dedication are there, geographical disadvantages can be overcome. Indeed, Roger Taylor, Gerald Battrick and Mike Davies all proved this in recent years.

Champions become champions in spite of difficulties.

So far as learning the 'language' of tennis is concerned, no films had ever been made specifically for this until 1972. Then the official British journal *Lawn Tennis* added yet another 'first' to its ever growing list of major pioneering operations by producing a carefully conceived, six minute film titled 'Learn to read Tennis'.

This aims to give players who have limited opportunities of competing in or seeing top class play a vivid opportunity of watching nine of the world's greatest champions hitting shots as though from the opposite end of a court to the viewer. Logically, by watching and analysing the film repeatedly, a viewer will improve his tennis reading ability.

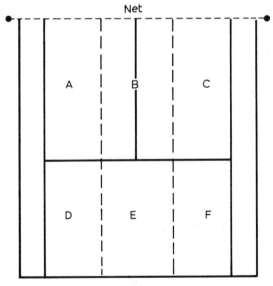

Fig. 64

To a lesser degree, some improvement can be made by carefully studying pictures and here is a test for you to take.

First, draw a diagram representing your half of a tennis court and divide it into rectangles as in Fig. 64.

Now study Figs. 65–69 and enter on your diagram where you think each ball landed after being hit.

Turn to page 98 for the answers.

Fig. 65

Fig. 66

Fig. 67

Fig. 68

Fig. 69

Scoring

10   =Excellent. Move on to suitable films as soon as you can. Practise 'reading' every time you practise on court. Make your practice as systematic as you can but it must be mobile. Avoid standing in one spot—say a corner—and hitting balls back and forth in one direction. Use sequences as detailed in my book *Match-Winning Tennis* (Faber and Faber).

9 or 8   =Good. Proceed as for 10 points but pay closer attention to details. Watch your opponents and 'practice partners' more objectively than at present.

7 or 6   =Fair only. You need to make a much closer study of tennis and your concentration is lacking. You need a lot of study and work.

5 or less =Read all you can about tennis. Watch good play as much as you can. When you do, watch the player rather than the ball going backwards and forwards across the net. You need lessons from a first class coach. If you do not know of one, write to *Lawn Tennis*, 'Lowlands', Wenhaston, Suffolk IP19-9DY, enclosing a s.a.e. for reply.

Answers

The answers to the test on pages 96–7 are: Figs. 65, 66, 67, 68 — rectangle F; Fig. 69—rectangle D. Score 2 for each correct answer, 1 if you are in adjoining rectangle.

What are the signs? In the case of Fig. 65 the player's right leg is forward rather than across and his shoulder has turned too far into the ball for a cross court shot. The ball could be going to B or C but he is well forward in the court and the face of his racket is vertical rather than under the ball as for a slice. Therefore the shot will be deep and the ball will land somewhere in F.

In Fig. 66 the stance is open but his right shoulder and right wrist are both back rather than forward. He is also on the service line and there is no evidence of slice. Could be E or C but the shoulder and wrist mark it as F.

Fig. 67 is, clearly, an overhead smash. The angle and tilt of the racket face and the poise of the body show the hit has to be cross court and deep so F must be the area.

Fig. 68 shows the right leg well across, the racket face tilting upwards and towards the sideline a direction confirmed by his eyes. The ball must fall in F. Fig. 69 shows the wrist and shoulder well back, the feet close together and the head poised for a straight drive. The swing back has been powerful and there is no suggestion of heavy top spin to make the ball dip. It must fall in D.

Chapter Seven

The Intangibles

How much do champions owe to heredity or inborn qualities? In fact, the percentage of sons who have achieved similar success to that of their fathers or mothers is negligible. In Britain there are just two, John Paish (1971) the son of Geoffrey Paish (1947) and Christopher Mottram (1972) son of Tony Mottram (1947). All were chosen for Britain's Davis Cup team. No former Wimbledon men's singles winner has been emulated by his son.

On the other hand, there are many instances of brothers achieving equal eminence. For example, the Renshaw, Baddeley and Doherty brothers all won the singles at Wimbledon while in the intense competition of the 1960s the Fraser brothers, Neale and John, won the singles and reached the quarter-finals respectively. Strangely, however, there have been few instances of sisters achieving greatness although the Trumans, Christine and Nell, represented Britain in the Wightman Cup.

Nevertheless, subjective views of many great achievers in sport suggest there are marked and similar characteristics of greatness among so many successful participants that one inevitably concludes there are genetic influences at work. It seems that the 'greatness' genes influence success in a number of possible fields and that environmental factors lead to individual adoptions of tennis rather than cricket or banking or soldiering or . . . ? This reasoning has been supported more objectively by Professor David McClelland of the Psychology faculty at Harvard University. He has isolated a personality factor which has been labelled 'the Self Motivated Urge to Achieve' and recorded scientifically by the symbol 'N.Ach'.

This recognises that certain individuals possess an inborn drive or necessity to do whatever task they undertake to the very limits of their capabilities, irrespective of any tangible reward that may follow. So, whether it is building a bridge, playing an instrument, sweeping a road, or participating in a game, they have only one standard of performance—the best of which they are capable.

McClelland has devised systems for measuring or assessing a person's N.Ach quotient and, more importantly, conceived techniques which can increase the factor in people who do not rate highly on tests or in dynamic life situations. In passing, British people are far down the world league as an ethnic group, not that America rates especially high. So far as Britain is concerned, my personal view is that we are a supremely humane race and that this has, over the generations, channelled our drives into other pools of behaviour.

Be that as it may, men with high N.Ach content exhibit certain well defined characteristics. For example, they are constantly setting challenges for themselves and then assessing success versus failure after attempting to overcome them. In attacking these challenges they display a carefully judged balance between adventure and care.

Tests can measure this quality of judgment. For example, in one set by Professor McClelland the subject is handed half a dozen hoops of the type found at a fairground hoop-la stall and instructed to throw as many as possible over a peg. 'You may stand wherever you like,' he is told.

The cautious, non-accepter of challengers will normally move close, the unsound gambler retreat too far away. The high N.Ach man can be observed mentally assessing a balance between challenge and success.

Here is another example for the long battery of tests needed for the complete assessment; the subject is seeking all the time for high marks. Try it out yourself.

For ten marks, choose between cutting a pack of playing cards once and turning up an ace, king, queen or jack or, after five seconds pause when you have read the following problem, attempting to solve it in three minutes.

Do not cheat because only you will suffer. Remember, you have five seconds to choose between trying to cut ace, king, queen or jack or attempting to solve the problem which is: 'A hunter for food set out from his home and travelled 6 miles due south. He then saw a bear, tracked it 3 miles due east and then shot it. Because the bear was very large, he decided to measure his distance from home. It was 6 miles'.

What was the colour of the bear? Dot, dot, dot, dot, dot, DECIDE Now, cut or problem.

The answer is on page 118.

Hand in glove with high N.Ach goes strong frustration tolerance, and techniques for assessing this were used with great success in the training of RAF pilots during World War II. Such tests tend to be elaborate, as are others which measure persistence.

Creativity and imagination tend to correlate with N.Ach and, again, there are techniques for measuring these factors.

Inherent self-confidence is important so test yourself on this factor by drawing a picture in this rectangle, making use of the squiggle already there.

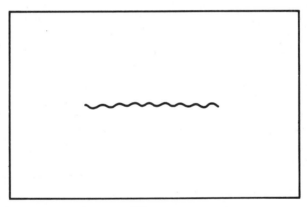

Fig. 70

For an interpretation of your result see page 118.

Control of nervousness is important.

Here I must emphasise that the tests in this book are very elementary and must not be taken too seriously. Nevertheless, they do give a slight inkling of the truth and should set you thinking along lines leading to improved achievement.

Today there is growing evidence that we can change our attitudes by positive action. This is well expressed by the famous plastic surgeon Maxwell Maltz, MD, FICS, in his book *Psycho-Cybernetics* (Pocket Books, U.S.A.). In a nusell, he postulates that we always act in accordance with our self-image; indeed, we are incapable of anything else. The self-image is governed by the subconscious mind but this, he asserts, is not a 'mind' at all but a 'servo-mechanism' consisting of the brain and nervous system which is used by and directed by the mind.

Consequently, disciplined, positive use of the mind can set this servo-mechanism working purposefully to help achievement of a specific goal. And as man has evolved to a state in which he possesses creative imagination, he is adequately equipped to 'think' his way to greater heights of achievement. This involves use of 'mental rehearsal' techniques as described in my earlier book *Tennis: How to Become a Champion* (Faber).

High drive is an important factor in success but such ergic tension mingles with nervousness and this is a constant worry with tennis players.

Seeking to discover more about this, I carried out some 'field' investigations back in 1970 and then wrote of the findings in the March 1971 issue of *Lawn Tennis*.

The article read:

It's your first match of the tournament season and as you wait to go on court your legs feel leaden. On court your right arm and elbow are tense, your breathing is difficult, and your stroke play tentative. In a nutshell, you are nervous.

Probably you will worry and wish the nervousness would vanish. Down at the other end of the court your opponent looks composed and certain, almost enviably so. You may think to yourself, 'why am I so afflicted'. Maybe you will take this worry home within yourself, perhaps to disturb your sleep. In the long term you may even become markedly depressive about this, to you, unwelcome facet of your personality—or temperament if you prefer the popular word.

Take heart, you are far from alone. Your companions in nervousness include many of the most famous names in the game, as a research into nervousness carried out by this magazine last year proved somewhat startlingly.

Lawn Tennis magazine investigators questioned in detail 33 top class tournament competitors and, believe it or not, 32 of them revealed that they suffer nervousness before and during important tournament matches.

Indeed, four of the very best asserted that they wished to be nervous for only then were they really keyed up for peak effort. The four: Rod Laver, Tony Roche, Margaret Court and Billie-Jean King.

The complete list of players investigated was that quartet plus Roger Taylor, Andres Gimeno, Cliff Drysdale, Dick Crealy, Clark Graebner, Charles Pasarell, Arthur Ashe, Manuel Santana, Juan Gisbert, Koji Watanabe, Jan Kodes, Patrice Beust, Allan Stone, Terry Addison, Barry Phillips-Moore, Jim McManus and Martin Mulligan. The women were Evonne Goolagong, Françoise Durr, Mary Ann Curtis, Julie Heldman, Peaches Bartkowicz, Kathy Harter, Kristy Pigeon, Shirley Brasher, Ceci Martinez, Esme Emanuel, Kazuko Sawamatsu, Judy Dalton, Helga Niessen, Madelaine Pegel, Gail Chanfreau, Carole Kalegeropolous and Christiane Spinoza.

To isolate the one player who claims never to suffer from nervousness, he is Martin Mulligan.

The first object of the research was to try to unearth the reasons why players become nervous and these turned out to be manifold. The table is as follows. The fact that the total exceeds 33 is because many players listed more than one reason for personal nervousness.

REASONS FOR NERVOUSNESS

Fear of playing badly . . . 17; Wanting the honour of the Title . . . 11; Fear of letting down country or team . . . 11; Fear that physical condition was not good enough . . . 7; Fear strokes would not stand up . . . 7; Fear of losing to someone slightly weaker and so of losing 'face' . . . 6; Because of not practising and training well enough . . . 6; Fear of letting down parents or friends . . . 5; Fear of wasting time playing tennis instead of, say study . . . 5; Needed the cash prize . . . 4; Fear of making a fool of self . . . 4; Fear of not giving opponent a good game . . . 3; Fear that defeat might mean loss of invitations for teams or tournaments . . . 3; 'It's natural' . . . 1; 'When I think I can win' . . . 1.

Rod Laver was the champion in this. He said, 'I suffer from a combination of all. But I don't want to lose it as I play well when I am keyed up and nervous'.

The next thing to discover was how long the nervousness lasts or when it strikes. The table came out: Varies . . . 6; The warm up . . . 6; First few games . . . 11; First set . . . 3; Whole match . . . 4; At end of close match . . . 5; Just before match . . . 1.

The excess of answers over subjects comes from cases where players suffer nervousness at more than one stage of a match.

Nervousness affects the subjects in a variety of ways and many players suffer multiple symptoms. Breathlessness . . . 4; Leaden legged . . . 12; Legs tense . . . 3; Legs weak . . . 1; 'Steel elbow' . . . 6; Cannot see properly . . . 3; Excessively irritable . . . 5; Cannot think . . . 1; Court seems too small . . . 1; Stomach butterflies . . . 6; Excessive sweating . . . 2; Feel tired . . . 2; Feel weak . . . 1; Shake . . . 1; Want to get off court as quickly as possible . . . 1; Heart beat increases . . . 1; Become tentative . . . 5; Become impulsive and rash . . . 2; Indifferent . . . 1; Court seems too big . . . 1; Think too much . . . 1; Forehand becomes shaky . . . 1; Service toss up goes wrong . . . 1; Stay back or, alternatively, rush net on every shot . . . 1; Hit too hard or too softly . . . 1; Hit ball too early or too late . . . 1; Lunge at ball instead of moving feet . . . 1.

How do players tackle the problem of nervousness? Here are some of the methods and answers. **Tony Roche:** 'It's good to be nervous. Get on with the game, become immersed in it and forget.'

Julie Heldman: 'Run as much as possible, try not to go for winners too early, watch the opponent's toss on service.'

Peaches Bartkowicz: 'Try to get a good lead. Keep on toes. Always moving.'

Clifford Drysdale: 'Concentrate hard.'

Kathy Harter: 'Concentrate specifically on what I want to do with the ball.'

Kristy Pigeon: 'The more nervous I become the better I play and concentrate. So I try to get nervous but rarely succeed.'

Esme Emanuel: 'Watch the ball.'

Clark Graebner: 'Get on with the game.'

Charles Pasarell, Barry Phillips-Moore, Carole Kalegeropolous: 'Take deep breaths.' (P-Moore: 'and take time.')

Arthur Ashe: 'Relax. The sun will still shine tomorrow whatever happens.'

Juan Gisbert: 'Hit the ball very hard even if it goes out.'

Judy Dalton: 'Watch the ball and keep it in play.'

Jim McManus: 'Concentrate on the court.'

Rod Laver: 'Don't want to lose nervousness as it makes me play well. Keep moving feet, talk to myself, just think of hitting the ball back.'

FULLER UNDERSTANDING

For a fuller understanding of personality it is necessary to read 'Personality traits in tennis players' by John Kane and John Callaghan in the July 1965 issue of this magazine or the relative chapters in my book *Tennis: How to Become a Champion*. The magazine is now sold out but for those interested photostat copies of the article can be supplied at 15p, inclusive of postage.

The particularly relevant passage in the article reads. 'However, on two primary factors the groups (World "top-twenty" rankers and very good tournament players) were very different. The discriminating factors were F (Surgency-uncontrolled elation) and Q4 (Tenseness) in which the tournament players were significantly higher.

'High surgency is very common among track and field athletes but it seems that first class players (tennis) need to be nearer the general population mean.

'The high Q4 scoring of the tournament players would indicate that many of these players have not developed the ego strength necessary to cope with the energy excitement generated in the game. . . .'

Elsewhere the article reads: 'Apparently for success in tennis a little basic temperamental anxiety may be useful so long as it can be controlled by compensating personality traits'.

Of these ego strength appears the most important. In the Handbook for the 'Sixteen Personality Factor Questionnaire' by Raymond B. Cattell, PhD, DSc, and Herbert W. Eber, PhD—Institute for Personality and Ability Testing, Illinois—the factors indicative of ego strength are listed: 'Emotionally mature and stable, calm, phlegmatic, realistic about life, absence of neurotic fatigue, placid.'

The other end of the continuum lists 'lacking in frustration tolerance, changeable (in attitudes), showing general emotionality, evasive (on awkward issues and facing personal decisions), neurotically fatigued, worrying'.

The factor is said to be approximately 80 per cent hereditary and 20 per cent due to environment.

However, I hold research proof that some players have improved their ego strength by as much as three standard deviations—a tremendous jump—over a five-year period. They are players who took part in the original research and have been measured again during the past nine months.

Five years may seem a long time but it isn't really when a youngster is aiming for the top. It can be done but it demands strong and persistent mental effort.

So, if you are nervous, realise this can be an asset. The champions make it work for them. If you are to emulate them you, too, must learn to harness your nervousness. How? Each man to his choice. Personally, I believe Laver and Roche show the way in their answers and I like Ashe's philosophy.

YOUR TEST—FIRST COMPLETE THIS QUESTIONNAIRE

The manifestations of ego strength are subtle and not always easily identifiable. The following quiz will give you an approximate —repeat approximate—idea of your own rating. It is intended for guidance and must not be considered a final and definite assessment. On the other hand, the test is basically sound.

Since the quiz is intended to help you, do not stupidly cheat yourself. Answer the questions as truthfully as you can by underlining the answer nearest to your feelings about yourself.

(1) I suffer somewhat from claustrophobia.
    (a) occasionally, (b) never, (c) rarely.
(2) I find myself repeatedly worrying over trivialities.
    (a) yes, (b) occasionally, (c) never.
(3) My parents are understanding when I have to make difficult decisions.
    (a) yes, (b) moderately, (c) no.
(4) I would like to change my life for one which is less demanding.
    (a) yes, (b) not sure, (c) no.
(5) The tones in which people say things hurt me more than the actual words they use.
    (a) true, (b) in between, (c) false.
(b) I find habits comparatively easy to change.
    (a) yes, (b) no, (c) uncertain.
(7) I find life in the 1970s full of frustrations and restrictions.
    (a) yes, (b) in between, (c) no.
(8) The weather has little effect on my mood and performance.
    (a) yes, (b) no, (c) in between.
Now turn to the key on page 118.

WINNING ATTITUDES

As a man thinks, so he is. To that extent winning attitudes can become habitual just as much as a losing mentality can become ingrained. So, from the very start, cultivate a positive, inquisitive, 'get up and go' outlook.

There is a growing belief today that what is generally known as the subconscious is, in fact, a 'servo-mechanism' which guides us towards the goals set by ourselves through our conceptions of self —by our ego in the language of psychology.

Firstly, then, one must acquire familiarity with techniques for developing a realistic understanding of one's capabilities—and of constantly increasing and improving those capabilities.

It is known that hypnosis cannot force a man to act against his basic beliefs or to perform tasks which are outside his capacities. For example, a man who habitually slices his backhand ground shot and has never attempted to hit the ball with top spin cannot be hypnotised into hitting streams of perfect top spin backhand drives. On the other hand, if he has developed a sound top spin technique in practice which becomes inhibited under the stress of competition, hypnotism can remove or alleviate the stress factor and thus allow the subject to perform the shot as effectively in competition as on the practice court. But one doesn't need hypnotism.

Pause for a moment, put down this book, and point your two forefingers approximately at one another about 18 inches in front of your nose. Do this for about 10 to 15 seconds and then pick up the book again. Right, start now.

You've done this? How were those fingers? Steady as a rock, I fancy. Now find a needle and a reel of cotton and try to thread the cotton through the eye of the needle in 10 to 15 seconds. What about those hands now? Unless you are a natural 'winner' they will have a considerable shake.

Yet what is the true difference in the situation? None really, except that you have applied pressure to yourself and tried too hard. To improve in tennis technique, remember that little experiment. Then set about grooving your strokes so that they can be performed over and over again without any breakdown of the acquired skill. Arrange for a friend or coach to feed you thousands of balls in short spells, day after day, week after week, throughout the winter.

Begin each session with simple feeding that applies no pressure. As each session progresses, have the pressure increased but strive above all to retain the basic groove or skill. As confidence grows, let that pressure become ever heavier.

If possible, obtain the use of a ball firing machine because it can bombard you with strings of 'drives' which even Laver could not rival. Do not fall into the trap of merely returning those balls anywhere in court. Aim for one or the other line—aiming for lines instead of the centre of the court is purely a matter of habit which can be formed by exercising mental discipline in the early days.

Concurrently with the physical, on court, practice, train yourself in mental rehearsal by thinking positively. Use the 'servo-mechanism' conception of the subconscious by vivid imaginings of the ball travelling as you wish through striking it in absolute accord with your ideal stroke. Let that picture burn itself into your mind. See the ball flash across the net before arrowing straight to the target. This practice should (a) develop the technical efficiency and consistency of the stroke and (b) so inculcate a feeling of confidence in the player.

Concurrently, he should be acquiring a degree of relaxation and a philosophy of 'doing my best and accepting victory or defeat with equanimity'. This lines up with the theory of 'par tennis' which I formulated many years ago.

In brief, this states that during a normal competitive season you will meet a number of opponents who are markedly either your superior or your inferior. Your very best form will not be good enough to beat the former. Your poorest efforts will be too good for the latter group.

There will also be a few—perhaps six, maybe ten—of similar standard to yourself. These you must beat. Once actually on a court, most of us play within narrow limits of our capabilities 90 per cent of the time. On 8 per cent of our matches we play well below average and only in about 2 per cent will we hit a super streak.

Normally when meeting vastly superior opponents, youngsters strive to make shots and use tactics far beyond their capabilities. From the preceding paragraph, the chance of any kind of success is only about one in fifty. Few gamblers would accept such odds. So it seems wiser always to strive for one's best—'par'—form in match play, to note carefully where it is inadequate, and then to set about rectifying those inadequacies on the practice court.

This is clearly wise on a long term basis and is less negative, when related to meeting strong opponents, than might be realised. A superior player will expect to win easily and so may be marginally slack. Thus you should escape the trap of trying to do too much, so conceding an inordinately high percentage of errors and making an opponent's easy task even easier.

Additionally, the rallies will become shorter and the chance will be less of becoming accustomed to the more intense pressure imposed by a superior player.

Now consider the policy of trying to play your normal game, quietly and without fear of losing by a bad score or of being made to look foolish. In this relaxed frame of mind you will have a better chance of enjoying the rallies. Your opponent, forced to make winning shots because you are not conceding strings of cheap errors, may start making a few more mistakes himself. As the match progresses you will find yourself handling his pace and depth a shade more confidently. If you cling on—'stay with him'—long enough he may become fractionally irritated and his form deteriorate in consequence.

Most of the time you will still lose, but often by, say, 6–2 6–3 instead of 6–1 6–2. Perhaps once a year you will spring a major upset.

More importantly, you will strengthen your ability to play par tennis and so increase your chances of developing a sound match winning temperament.

You will also learn much more about the ways you must strengthen your game in order to advance another rung up the ladder. The journey to fulfilment is made up of many small steps accompanied by intense quality of thought and effort. Striving always to find one's best form in matches, while seeking energetically and constantly to raise the level of that best, is theoretically sound and practically advisable. It is vastly superior to wild attempts suddenly to play like a Laver on a few occasions each competitive season. Even it this possesses a heady excitement, it is a gamble, and true champions are seldom compulsive gamblers. They like to have all their affairs under personal control.

TOTAL COMMITMENT

Television viewers who saw on BBC 2 the final of 1966 in which Pancho Gonzales beat Rod Laver 6–3, 5–7, 12–10 are unlikely ever to forget the irresistible will to win shown then by the ageing Pancho.

Out on his feet half an hour before the match ended, he exercised remarkable self-discipline in husbanding negligible reserves of stamina.

Not by 1 yard would he deviate to collect a stray ball. Nor would he bend by a degree to pick one up. Only returns within reach did he strive to play, except on key points.

His economy of effort in holding his own service games neared 100 per cent in efficiency. His first deliveries found their target on point after point and his following volley might have been computer calculated, so precisely did the ball explore the area which caused Laver the greatest difficulty.

There came one dubious decision and he flared. . . . But he quickly quelled the outburst. He had energy to spare only for winning; not for quarrelling over lost causes.

'You could have lost with honour ages ago. Why didn't you quit?' he was asked.

'When you have tried so hard for so long it would be a waste of all that effort not to go on trying to the end', he replied.

'When you are so tired how can you keep going?', came the supplementary question.

'I guess someone helps you,' he explained, an obvious point made even clearer after his epic win over Charles Pasarell after saving seven match points in the 1969 Wimbledon Open. Asked if he prayed during that match, he answered, 'Yes, I guess all players do.'

Change the scene to an underground table tennis club in New York where Murray Deloford and I were striving against one another for a 'quarter' bet back in 1937.

On the next table the local 'Flash Harry' was disposing of cronies, the while insulting 'Limeys' in general and us in particular. Finally he challenged Deloford and the battle began before an audience of about ten.

Point by point they edged tensely towards 21. The rallies were long and fast and neither seemed willing to yield. 15–All, 16–all, 17–all was called.

Then, at 18–all, 'Flash' started asides to his pals, trying, perhaps, to imply that, really, the match meant nothing.

The rallies were still long but Deloford's will was the stronger. He won 21–19 and as we climbed the stairs Deloford said, 'When he started talking I knew he had quit.'

Some years ago I found myself 2–5 and love–forty down in the final set of a singles semi-final. Serving and running in, I heard the call 'fault' and began my trudge back.

Turning, I saw my opponent had moved well over in order to clobber my second serve with his forehand. So I reasoned, 'If I ace him he'll be so shocked he'll miss the next point as well and I'll only have to fight really hard for one of the match points.'

A double fault would, of course, have ended it all but the ball sped down the middle line untouched. Shaken, he missed the next return and when I ran in on the third match point he missed the sideline.

I took the set 7–5 and on leaving the court I was bombarded with questions like 'but supposing you had double-faulted?' I did not linger to explain. Yet how I would have been slated if it had been a double fault.

These seemingly unrelated incidents contain a common factor which, I believe, shows why people of equal skills and talents can differ so widely in achievement. Think momentarily of Angela Mortimer Barrett and her reaction to bad calls. 'That's one point you shouldn't have won. I'll make sure it isn't two,' she used to resolve while redoubling her efforts to win the next point.

That factor is total commitment to victory.

Contrast it with some players you know or have seen who blow up in face of dubious calls or net cords, wasting valuable nerve and energy on futile demonstrations, arguments, asides to the crowds and so on.

In the instances outlined above not one tiny bit of holding back or reserve existed. Loss of dignity through chasing but failing, or having to withstand barrages of criticisms and demands to know 'why did you do it' or building up an alibi—'She was so lucky, how could I have won?'—simply did not enter into the reckonings. The one quitter, 'Flash Harry', lost.

Even harder than acknowledging to others that one has put one's all into winning and yet lost is acknowledging it to oneself. Who amongst us does not try to save face with himself? It is less comfortable to face reality than to find an excuse for failure.

Maybe the opponent did have a wicked net cord and a ghastly line call at 4–all in the final set but how many extra points will you yield because of them?

In that moment you accept the easy alibi, quit and tell yourself later, 'I had him until he got the net cord and bad call. How can you win against that kind of luck?' And even if you try not to think that way, you know in your subconscious that your pals will say it for you afterwards.

It is uncomfortable utterly to reject the alibi, to flog one's weary body and mind for another agonising twenty minutes and still lose. Because if one has truly rejected the alibi one cannot later recall it.

Yet only through total commitment can one surmount all hurdles and reach the limits of one's potential. There is no room for dignity, postures, façades and the like. The common 'how can I play so badly?' words and gestures which follow so many mistakes never arise; the mind and spirit are far too occupied with factors relevant to the match even to be diverted to such irrelevant trivia.

To repeat, defeats become more painful. . . . Yet also more valuable and, in some degree, exciting or stimulating. Absolute self-honesty works both ways. One loses but sees truly the steps which have to be climbed in order to reach and pass one's conqueror. The ways to do this become apparent. The challenge of achievement becomes vivid and exciting.

Total commitment, one learns quickly, is not confined simply to matches on court. It invades practice and training, permeates moments of relaxation and takes up residence in one's home.

Frankly, I doubt if words can convey the feeling to the psyche of any man or woman who is not genetically endowed with the facets of personality which create this attitude to competition. I can offer six pieces of practical advice. Shun all alibis, especially in yourself. Banish stupid pride and unnatural behavioural attitudes. Go all out to win and think only of winning until the last point is over. No matter what the demands on your self-discipline, disregard net cords and bad calls. 'Stay' with your opponent on every stroke on every point in every game of each set. Enjoy the battle for the sake of the battle, trusting that victory will come in the end, even if that end is four hours ahead.

PLANNING A WINTER PROGRAMME

Success in tennis nowadays entails complete dedication and effort. Ideally a young man should practise and train 5 days a week during those precious winter months when improvement is normally achieved.

On the whole I believe each individual should plan his own programme in consultation with a coach. Frequently this is not possible.

So at risk of prescribing a winter schedule which will leave me open to the charge of 'turning out uniform robots', here is one well-thought-out programme.

It was devised by Eddy King, the LTA Regional Coach, and published in the April 1971 issue of *Lawn Tennis*. It reads:

As a Physical Training Educationalist I have consistently attended progressive and advanced courses, seminars, conferences, lectures etc, concerned with all aspects of coaching—psychology, physiology, technical and so on—and I can fairly claim that I specialise in modern training techniques. These I have been applying to a small group of young men during a vigorous, full-time training programme spread over the entire winter and designed to achieve the greatest possible advance in time for the start of the 1971 season. The squad are now facing the acid test of success or failure in the first of their season's tournaments.

Much interest has been shown in the training methods and it is in the hope that they may benefit keen-to-improve youngsters that I now put them down on paper.

We work to a 20 hours per week programme and I wish to make one thing absolutely clear from the start.

It is THERE IS NO SUBSTITUTE FOR SKILL. Enthusiasm, guts, the sheer will to work, physical fitness may enable quite moderately skilled performers to attain high standards but, to some degree, it could be claimed that any success they gain is in spite of their moderate skills. Those qualities are essential and each member of the squad has worked with dedication to develop them. But, in the end, they achieve more if skills are high, just as the skilled performer must attend to the imponderables if he is to achieve full potential.

It must also be remembered that when tiredness of body and mind creeps in skills normally deteriorate. My course has accepted these criteria and the breakdown of time has been approximately 15 hours skills development, 5 hours physical fitness. But many of the skills sessions contain a deliberately high quota of fitness training: modern teaching acknowledges that the amount of transfer of exercises to actual playing techniques or systems is severely limited, no matter how closely the exercises simulate the playing situation. And so to the course.

Each day the five youths—Robin Drysdale, Philip Siviter, Ashley Compton-Dando, Chris Revell and Gary Dudic—spend about 4 hours on the court and 1 hour in physical training. On court during September and October the programme was (1) individual work on technical faults and modification of stroke production; (2) good length rallying establishing records and counting only returns which fall between the service and baselines; (3) constant practice to groove all strokes; (4) competitive practices but very few games played.

November and December: In addition to the above, (1) pressure training activities, two and three against one for groundstroke, volley and overhead work; (2) conditioned games. Example, more points lost for unforced errors than gained for outright winners.

January and February: emphasis on match play with special attention to concentration, pacing, specific tactics, vital points, crisis moments, etc.

March: the squad will be competing in the French tournaments under my personal supervision who, as their manager, will analyse their match play and conduct a training programme around the tournaments.

September and November: Stamina training; 3 mile timed runs

increasing to 5 mile timed runs on grass. Weight training; basic training schedules designed to build up each player's strengths and to accustom him to handling weights. Six basic weight training exercises designed to exercise the large muscle groups of the body. Examples: shoulders, arms, stomach, legs. Fairly light weights are used, example: 40 lb increasing to 60 lb and from 10 to 15 repetitions.

Circuit training: basic circuit of eight activities performed twice each week and timed and recorded for each player. The intensity of this training has increased over the months.

December to February: gradually stamina training has been replaced by short runs with sprint bursts interspersed with slow running and walks. The sprints include forward and backward runs and are over distances of 30 to 40 yards.

Weight training: more specific exercises for tennis have been introduced during this period, the poundage has increased considerably, according to each individual's strength capacity.

Circuit training: this has continued once per week only.

The 45 seconds training on court is a specialised operation modified for tennis purposes. It is designed to combat fatigue and to improve recovery capacity by dispersing lactic acid which builds up during violent activity on the court. Players continually reproduce moments of on-court maximum activity through being fed a constant stream of returns in a pattern shown by the diagram; this is varied slightly from burst to burst and the two 'feeders' do not attempt to make their placements off the trainee's returns but hit dead balls which they hold in readiness.

Fig. 71 shows the 45 second maximum effort routine. The trainee serves at ace speed from S and races forward for a high backhand volley at HBV, on to LFV for low forehand volley, back to K for smash, up to touch net at TN, back for lob at L, over to FH for forehand, up to HBV again and so until 45 seconds is up.

Violent exercise is maintained for 45 seconds, followed by 45 seconds rest. The whole exercise is continued for 5-minute periods, building up to 12 minutes as the players develop the physical/physiological/mental capacities to endure it.

This exercise is based on the known fact that when performing all-out activities a man ejects 3 grammes of lactic acid per second

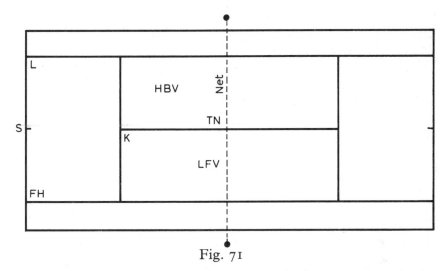

Fig. 71

into the blood stream. He can carry a total of 140 grammes in the system before collapsing. Simple mathematics show that 45 seconds of flat out activity take him near to the point of total collapse.

Potato races: various types of potato races, using tennis balls are included. The one shown in Fig. 72 is specifically used for timing. The player starts from S and runs to ball at each X, returning to S

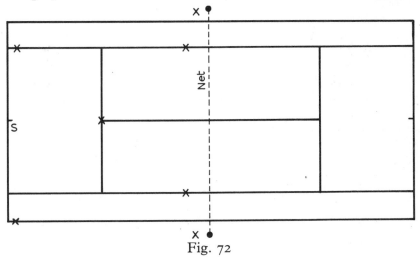

Fig. 72

backwards before putting ball in box. Personal records of times are kept by each player.

During the entire winter's programme fitness tests have been given regularly and weights checked carefully. The latest figures show that each player has made considerable progress and the group as a whole are in excellent physical conditions. The Harvard Step and Tuttle Pulse Ratio Tests were used.

ANSWER TO PROBLEM ON PAGE 100

The answer does not matter. The high N.Ach man normally seeks to control his own destiny and so leaves little to chance . . . and cutting the cards is a 16 out of 52 chance. So he will prefer the problem. Score 0 for cutting the cards, 10 for choosing the problem, whether or not you arrive at the correct answer which is 'white'. Why white? Only at the North Pole could those distances be true, and polar bears are white.

ANSWER TO DRAWING ON PAGE 101

If the whole of your picture is above the squiggle you are displaying 'confident' symptoms, especially if there is a sun in it.

If the whole of your picture is below the squiggle, the suggestion is of timidity. Half above and half below, etc., indicates the ratio between confidence and lack of it.

ANALYSIS OF REPLIES TO QUESTIONNAIRE ON PAGE 106

Question	Your Score	Question	Your Score
(1) a 0; b 2; c 1	....	(6) a 2; b 0; c 1	....
(2) a 0; b 1; c 2	....	(7) a 0; b 1; c 2	....
(3) a 2; b 1; c 0	....	(8) a 2; b 0; c 1	....
(4) a 1; b 2; c 0	....		————
(5) a 0; b 1; c 2	....	Total	————

Score 13 to 16. Your ego strength appears to be above average and you should be able, through application, to master most situations —including nervousness in sporting competition.

Score 10 to 12. Average ego strength. You should meet no undue difficulty in dealing with anxiety situations in competition though if you are strong in mental drive you may suffer nervousness fairly frequently.

Score 0 to 10. Below average ego strength and therefore, you should be watchful. If you are a teenager this may be a condition of your years and you could grow out of it. But Heaven helps those who help themselves. Take stock. Do you sink into a dream world all too often?

Do you frequently imagine yourself in imaginary conversations in which you rout the other person? Are you too busy being envious of others' success, or in finding alibis for your own shortcomings, to give 100 per cent effort to your own plans for improvement? Take another look at Arthur Ashe's words, accept you cannot do better than your best—and then strive to make today's best better than yesterday's, tomorrow's better than today's and so on. Tall oaks from little acorns grow—and in that way nervousness can be harnessed for your good.

Chapter Eight

Play at the Peaks

Maybe one day the precepts laid down in this book will help you to the great honour of representing your country in the Davis Cup. This is a greater mental strain than playing at Wimbledon for in the first case you are bearing the responsibility of an entire country's reputation while in the latter only your personal prestige is at stake.

So as an exercise in the type of analysis you may some day need to undertake, study this report of someone else's first Davis Cup appearance. It appeared in *Lawn Tennis* and read:

On Friday 5th May 1972 David Lloyd, aged 24, made his Davis Cup debut. His opponent was Patrick Proisy of France; the venue, the slow, clay centre court at the Stade Roland Garros, Paris.

The temperature was moderate, the sun hazy and there was little or no wind. Around 600 people watched the match. Lloyd showed no signs of excessive nervousness except for a slight lacking in his usual dash. The 24 games that gave Proisy victory 6–1, 6–3, 6–2 lasted 100 minutes.

During that time they contested $44 + 50 + 64$ points, 158 in all and Lloyd hit $162 + 213 + 225$ shots, aggregating 600.

		Errors				Strokes per U.Error
	Unforced	Slight Pressure	Forced	Winners	Shots	
LLOYD						
SET 1	14	1	0	5	162	11·4
SET 2	17	1	1	6	213	11·8
SET 3	21	5	2	7	225	10·7
	—	—	—	—	—	
TOTALS	52	7	3	18	600	
PROISY						
SET 1	5	3	1	12	168	33·6
SET 2	12	3	1	9	210	17·5
SET 3	16	5	3	8	219	13·7
	—	—	—	—	—	
TOTALS	33	11	5	29	597	

Lloyd broke down at these stages:

Shot	SET 1	SET 2	SET 3
First	4	1	3
Second	3	6	6
Third	3	3	8
Fourth	3	2	5
Fifth	0	3	1
Sixth	1	1	2
Seventh	0	0	3
Ninth	0	1	0
Tenth	0	1	0
Eleventh	1	0	0
Thirtieth	0	1	0

Lloyd's errors in detail:
F=forehand, B=backhand, R=return of serve, V=volley, K=kill, DS=drop shot, L=lob, CC=cross court, DL=down line, P=passing shot, app=approach shot, ꝏ=reverse cross court, n after symbols=into net, s=out over sideline, b=out over baseline, ——— =game point saved, ∟___ =game, •=error under pressure, *=forced error. 2, etc.=Lloyd's shot in the rally.

SET 1.   BCCVb2; BRn1; ⌊FVn3; FCCPs4; BCCPn4;

FCCb3; BRn1; FCCPs3; BCCVb6; Fappb11;

BPDLn2; ⌊Fappn4; FDLn2; BRn1; FRn1

SET 2.   BLb6; Bn5; Fappb2; ⌊BPDLn10; BLb 2; BRn1;

Bn*3; FLƆɔs2; BPDLs4; FɔƆs2; FCCn30; Fb3;

Fn2; ⌊Fn4; Ks3; ⌊BCCVPn5; FƆɔb9; Bappn2;

⌊Bappb5.

SET 3.   FCCPb4; FRn1; FCCPs*2; Bn2; ⌊BPDLb7;

BDLs*4; Fappb7; Kb3; FPDLs•5; BVb4; FPDLn•6;

BRn•1; ⌊FɔƆs2; FCCb3; Fn2; FCCVn•4; FPDL•b2;

BRn1; BCCn3; FVn2; Fappb3; Fn3; ⌊FCCVs7; Kb3;

BPDLb6; BPDLb3; FƆƆPn3; ⌊BVn4.

Subjectively, the decisive factors appeared to be:
(1) Lloyd's limited stroke repertoire compared to Proisy.
(2) Lloyd's lack of penetration of stroke.
(3) Proisy's superior consistency helped by his use of spin.
(4) Proisy's greater penetration when attacking or countering helped significantly by taking ball on rise or at top of bounce. Use of 'through the ball' slice kept his approach shots low, forcing Lloyd to dig ball from ankles, so making passes difficult.
(5) Lloyd's completely stereotyped tactics. Virtually used *no* imagination.

To many, Davis Cup representation is the height of their tennis ambitions but some strive to rise above even that great level and a few achieve ultimate greatness—tennis immortality.

Rod Laver and Ken Rosewall are two such men and it is fitting, perhaps, that they should have contested one of the five greatest matches in the history of the game; it could even have been the greatest but such judgments of necessity must be subjective. Nevertheless, analyses and statistics are not subjective but factual.

Their epic took place on 14th May 1972 in the Moody Coliseum, Dallas, before 7,800 spectators. The first prize included $50,000, a Ford Lincoln car, a diamond bracelet for the wife and the title 'World Championship of Tennis' winner. The loser was not forgotten, a cheque for $20,000 providing financial solace though pride has no price.

The match lasted 3 hours 34 minutes and the NBC of America had allocated 2 hours of television time to cover. They scrapped all following programmes to maintain transmission to the end, something almost unprecedented on America's minutely timed, heavily financially weighted television networks.

Rosewall opened the match by serving to the backhand, running in and volleying across the court, Laver then erring with a lob.

It ended with Rosewall serving to the backhand, running in and Laver netting the return of service.

The analysis of all play broke down into:

Rosewall v. Laver
Summary of points won and lost on first and second services

SET		FIRST WON	FIRST LOST	SECOND WON	SECOND LOST
1	Rosewall	9	3	7	7
2		10	5	6	5
3		17	8	6	3
4		15	6	8	5
5		16	5	15	10
	TOTALS	67	27	42	30
1	Laver	11	7	10	9
2		1	10	9	7
3		9	5	6	5
4		12	7	12	4
5		20	11	11	11
	TOTALS	53	40	48	36

Rosewall v. Laver

Rosewall			ERRORS			
SET	Forced*	Pressure	Unforced	Unlucky	Winners	Shots
1	2	7	11	1	15	138
2	0	8	6	1	9	98
3	3	5	4	1	12	102
4	2	4	14	1	8	139
5	0	9	18	0	19	192
Totals	7	33	53	4	63	669
Laver						
1	0	5	9	1	12	148
2	0	9	14	1	5	100
3	0	11	10	0	13	99
4	0	4	17	4	15	146
5	2	7	24	0	20	193
Totals	2	36	74	6	65	686

Concentration Factor

(Number of shots hit in relation to number of unforced errors)

SET						
1	Rosewall 138–11	1–12·5		Laver 148– 9	1–16·4
2	98– 6	1–16·3		100–14	1– 7·1
3	102– 4	1–25·5		99–10	1– 9·9
4	139–14	1– 9·99		146–17	1– 8·6
5	192–18	1–10·7		193–24	1– 8·0
	669–53			686–74	

*Forced errors are those conceded when the chances of returning the ball into court are less than $33\frac{1}{3}$ per cent. Pressure errors are those made where, despite pressure, the chances of a successful return are better than even. Unforced errors should not have been. Unlucky errors cover fine shots which just go wrong, e.g. a great approach shot which clears the baseline by an inch.

They say that money is the great God of the professionals and it would be idle to pretend that financial rewards do not count.

Yet when Rosewall went up to receive the symbolic Cup and other winner's rewards he was so emotionally choked he could not speak.

When he returned to the locker room to shower and change into street clothes he put the $50,000 on a chair. Not until he reached his hotel did he again think of the money; a friend drove hurriedly back to recover the forgotten cheque.

As with most beginners, when the chips are really down, Rosewall thinks only of the game. In that lies the secret of his success.

Chapter Nine

Training, Fitness, Action and Reaction

Efficiency in physical activity is a function of the muscles and a muscle, in effect, is a factory which produces mechanical action.

To do this it must be fed with fuel—chemical fuel—which can be converted into muscle-contracting energy.

Muscle is made up of around 70 per cent water, 20 per cent protein and 10 per cent chemicals. In order to function efficiently it must be fed with two particular chemicals, glucose and oxygen. These are carried to the muscle through the blood vessels, at the centre of which is that superb muscular pump, the heart.

Oxygen is taken into the lungs via the normal process of breathing where it is caught up in the blood stream and pumped to the muscle by the action of the heart via arteries, arterioles and capillaries.

Arteries are large diameter tubes which carry the blood away from the heart. These channel off into smaller diameter vessels called arterioles which, in turn, feed the minute capillaries which lie alongside the muscle.

Fluids seep easily from the capillaries into the muscle, thus feeding it with the oxygen it requires and also the glucose, which comes from the liver. The blood, flowing on in the capillaries, returns to the heart via veins and then back to the lungs.

Muscle contraction uses up energy and this results in oxygen being converted into carbon dioxide which escapes into the veins and so to the lungs from where it is expelled through exhalation.

So efficient working of a muscle depends on an adequate supply of oxygen and glucose and rapid disposal of carbon dioxide.

If the oxygen supply is insufficient, lactic acid forms. This is

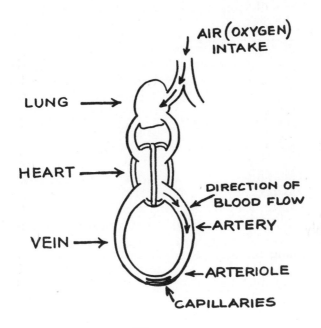

Fig. 73

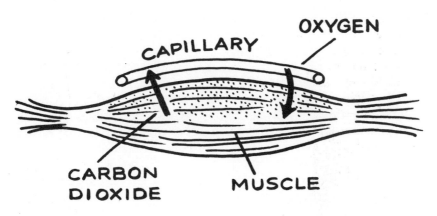

Fig. 74

poisonous and when it accumulates in the blood sets up the fatigue that limits ability to exercise and also reduces muscular skill.

100-metre sprinters often stop breathing in severe competitions and so run up a heavy oxygen debt which momentarily renders them semi-conscious though they quickly recover if fully fit. This situation seldom occurs in tennis.

So the primary objects of physical training should be to improve lung capacity and quality (so that more oxygen can be taken in per breath), to increase the heart's muscular size (and therefore, its pumping strength) and to develop smooth physical skills so that the muscle works ever less hard to achieve any given result.

The latter comes through the acquisition of good style, the former through well conceived, regular, purposeful training.

Technical (skill) improvement can often be assisted by well designed, specific exercises. For example, service power is vitally affected by wrist flexibility, so exercises which make the wrist more supple should (a) enable more service power to be generated and (b) permit that power to be maintained for a longer period of time before fatigue sets in.

Similarly, champions move quicker over the first two steps than lesser players. This is a factor of muscle explosive power which, in turn, is a function of power-weight ratio. So exercises which develop muscle strength without causing inflexibility and which, simultaneously, reduce body weight must assist motor acceleration.

On the whole muscle flexibility seems easier to achieve if the subject has taken part in good and varied exercise programmes before reaching the age of rapid growth, in early adolescence or, preferably, at primary school.

This is probably one reason why outdoor-orientated Australia abounds in splendid athletes and sports performers: the majority of its youngsters are actively engaged in all kinds of sporting activities from the moment they can walk.

Flexibility, so vital to success in tennis, is not a general factor; because one possesses flexible ankles one doesn't automatically have flexible knees and shoulders. So exercises have to be specific.

Specifics can scarcely be outlined in a book. Any reader determined to improve his performance should take up pen and paper and then go through a merciless self-analysis of his own physical factors: Is my right ankle as flexible as my left? How loose are my shoulders? Do I suffer any restriction of elbow movements? Do I move as quickly to the left as I do to the right, or vice versa? These are just a few of the questions he should ask himself.

Having answered with complete honesty—if you *must*, cheat other people but never, never yourself—persuade a knowledgeable friend to go through the paper with you. Then, having agreed on your weaknesses, think out specific exercises which can slowly convert those weaknesses into strengths. Consult an expert if in doubt, but always take final decisions yourself.

This cannot be overstressed. If you aim to become a champion —be it of your club, county or country—you are the one who has to make it come true. You will play the matches unaided. You will undergo the practice, purposefully, intelligently and with at least as much concentration as you would apply in a Wimbledon final because such finals are won on the practice court. And you will have to suffer and eventually come to relish the pain and suffering inseparable from intensive physical training. And if the training isn't intense, if it doesn't seem more testing and arduous than competitive tennis itself, it is probably not bringing much benefit.

However, always link training to tennis advancement. Nothing is more discouraging than training frantically and so greatly improving fitness, only to find that one's tennis form has stayed put or even gone backwards.

At such moments even the most devoted of men is likely to question the value of the entire campaign, even to quit. And the first time of quitting makes the second time just that much likelier and the third a fraction easier still.

The reason a tennis player trains is to increase tennis improvement. Keep that constantly in mind. Relate all training to tennis. Make extravagant use of specifics but keep in mind the limitations of transference.

I know of no better agility exercise than potato races because these involve starts, stops, turns and bends. Undoubtedly they improve court coverage but the thing they improve most of all is skill at potato races. So when, as I hope, you run such races, keep a vivid picture of a tennis court and match in your mind.

Such races can be run—against a stop watch—more or less anywhere but Fig. 75 shows one of many patterns which can be used on a tennis court.

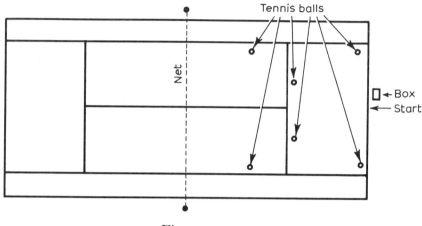

Fig. 75

Take a box of six tennis balls and place them as shown in the diagram, putting the box just off centre on the baseline. Start from the centre, running to each ball in turn, picking it up and returning it to the box.

If the balls are placed in precisely the same spots each time, it is possible to measure progress, via a stop watch, in the ever-reducing time it takes to return the six balls to the box. To obtain maximum benefit, use the right hand for one race, the left hand for another, and keep changing the direction of your turns so that you become equally proficient twisting to left or right.

Speed is extremely difficult to increase but stamina is relatively easy to improve.

The object of training is to match oxygen uptake in the blood and muscles and glucose supply with the muscle energy being expended. Far and away the best system for achieving this is running, just plain running, mile after mile of it.

Lifting a heavy weight just once, you expend a great deal of effort in a relatively short period of time. The effect is to increase strength.

In running you move only your body weight so in covering long distances you move your legs and arms many times when carrying only a light load. This increases stamina. Running flat out imposes a strain on the heart and lungs. The greater the change of stress running produces on the heart and lung action during training, the better performance will be later on.

How far and fast to run must be a personal decision. Istvan Gulyas, a world class player on clay courts though he is now over forty years old, runs five miles round the roads of Budapest four nights each week.

In running keep pushing up to and through the 'pain barrier' so that heart and lung capacity is constantly tested and extended. This can be brought about by interval running, e.g. 100 yards normal, 20 yards at sprint speed. Remember, to bring improvement training must hurt you.

Important as stamina may be, I personally rate it behind quickness in a champion's equipment. I have seen thirty-five Wimbledon men's singles finals and not once seen defeat directly attributable to stamina deficiency. On the other hand, superior speed of movement, especially over the first yard, was a vital factor in at least seventeen of those finals. So while you pound the roads building up invaluable stamina, make full use of the time and opportunity to increase your speed.

Physical speed must be allied to the anticipatory speed which comes through experience. Anticipation undoubtedly owes something to genetic factors but experience which leads to immediate recognition of repetitive situations exerts a much greater influence. Recognition of situations converts conceptual action into reflex action, so reducing the distance nerve impulses have to travel. And as normal nerve impulse pace has been measured at around 30 yards per second (W. Scott Murray, *Your body: how it is built and how it works*, Watts & Co., London) so a saving of one foot of travel represents a better than 1 per cent improvement in action time.

Situations become ingrained through actual play on court but constant watching of films and television, especially of semi-close-ups of the players, feeds the methods and patterns of players into viewers' minds; how many millions learned that soccer's immortal Stan Matthews always took opposing backs on the outside simply by repeatedly seeing him on television.

Watching plus education enables us to accept items of visual information in groups and so understand and use them more rapidly than when we can only take them item by item.

By working with films, especially those specifically designed for perceptual improvement by *Lawn Tennis,* the official journal of the Lawn Tennis Association, Barons Court, London, W14-9EG, you can improve your powers of recognition, anticipation and action.

Because of this, I refuse to accept the widely held notion that geographical location determines success. Obviously it is easier to practise and train if one lives near to an area which is rich in facilities, opposition and coaches.

But who can think of any champion who became pre-eminent in his field without intensive personal effort and self-sacrifice?

Coaching, financial sponsorship and inducements, well-wishing friends and associations have their uses, primarily—perhaps even exclusively—in producing increasing numbers of competent performers. Maybe any increase in the number of competent performers must push up top standards through the normal pressures of competition.

When it comes to actual champions only one thing really counts, the intensity and intelligence of personal effort. Only YOU can make YOU a champion. If you have that unbounded urge to achieve simply for the sheer satisfaction, you will read and re-read this and other books until the ink almost vanishes, even if you utterly reject most of the recommendations.

Champions may be born but the 'born' part is inspiration and we all know the formula for success, '10 per cent inspiration, 90 per cent perspiration'. So go and change into that playing kit immediately; time is far too precious to waste.